FOOTBALL FACTS

This Book Belongs To:

CONTENT

Round One : European Football

1. Which Turin-based Italian football club, often known as "La Vecchia Signora," secured their 27th Serie A title during the 2002-03 season?
a. Inter
b. Milan
c. Juventus
d. Roma

2. Among these Dutch players, recognized for his distinctive hairstyle, who never had a stint with Barcelona, one of Spain and Europe's most illustrious clubs?
a. Winston Bogarde
b. Johan Cruyff
c. Ruud Gullit
d. Ronald Koeman

3. Giovanni Ferrari, renowned as one of Italy's all-time great footballers, donned the jersey of which Italian club, perhaps evoking thoughts of a sausage akin to mortadella, during the 1940-1941 season?
a. Bologna
b. Fiorentina
c. Napoli
d. Vermicelli

4. Did Johan Cruyff, the iconic Dutch footballer, have a stint with any other Dutch club besides Ajax?
a. Yes
b. No

5. Paolo Montero, the Uruguayan footballer with a substantial European career, played primarily in which country, renowned for its delectable tomato-based cuisine, from 1992 to 2005?
a. Italy
b. France
c. Spain
d. Slovenia

6. Among German footballers Matthias Sammer, Jürgen Klinsmann, and Andreas Brehme, who had stints with the Italian club Inter Milan during their careers, Andreas Möller, on the contrary, had a brief period at Juventus between 1992 and 1994. For a substantial portion of his career, which other club, located in the city of his birth, did Möller play for?

a. First Vienna FC
b. Eintracht Frankfurt
c. Bayern Munich
d. VfB Stuttgart

7. **During his extensive career, Jean-Pierre Papin donned the jersey of numerous clubs. However, there is one "M" city, occasionally linked with casinos, where Papin never played. Which city is this?**

a. Monaco
b. Marseille
c. Milan
d. Munich

8. **The 1996 UEFA Champions League final featured a clash between Ajax and Juventus, and at half-time, the score was level at 1-1, courtesy of goals by Ravanelli and Litmanen. How was the match ultimately settled?**

a. Penalty shootout
b. Extra time
c. Golden goal
d. Coin toss

9. **Martin Palermo, the retired Argentine striker, had a stint with which Spanish club between 2001 and 2003, often referred to as the "yellow submarine" or "el submarino amarillo"?**

a. Boca Juniors
b. Villareal
c. Espanyol
d. Athletic Bilbao

10. **Zisis Vryzas, the forward who represented Perugia from 2000 to 2003, hails from which European nation of Hellenic origin, known for their victory over Portugal in the 2004 UEFA Euro final?**

a. Switzerland
b. Greece
c. Hungary
d. Austria

11. **Who clinched the Champions League title in 1999?**

a. Manchester United
b. Ajax Amsterdam
c. Barcelona
d. Bayern Munich

12. **Which country do the clubs of Galatasaray, Besiktas and Fenerbahce come from?**

a. Greece
b. Turkey
c. Israel
d. Germany

13. Gabriel Batistuta is a native of which South American Country?

a. Brazil
b. Paraguay
c. Chile
d. Argentina

14. In which city does Ajax play?

a. Amsterdam
b. The Hague
c. Rotterdam
d. Brussels

15. Who beat the Czech Republic in the Final of the 1996 European Championships?

a. Germany
b. Italy
c. France
d. Portugal

16. How many teams contest a group in the UEFA Champions League?

a. 3
b. 8
c. 5
d. 4

17. Italian Clubs were very successful in Europe in the 1990s, but how many clubs from Italy qualified for the quarterfinals of the UEFA cup in 2000?

a. 0
b. 2
c. 1
d. 3

18. The 'Old Firm Derby', is a clash between Rangers and Celtic, but which city do these teams hail from?

a. Edinburgh
b. Glasgow
c. Aberdeen
d. London

19.   Bray Wanderers, Bohemians, UCD and Kilkenny City, are all teams from which country?
a.   Scotland
b.   England
c.   Wales
d.   Ireland

20.   Which Spanish team won the first 5 European Cups?
a.   Imaginary Madrid
b.   Real Madrid
c.   Athletico Madrid
d.   Racing Madrid

21.   If a friend decides to watch the Gooners play against Liverpool, which team has your he/she gone to watch?
a.   Sheffield United
b.   Arsenal
c.   Gunport FC
d.   Tottenham Hotspur

22.   This Spanish club has employed legendary footballers such as Johann Cruyff and Lionel Messi, to mention just two. Which team is called the 'blaugrana'?
a.   Madrid
b.   Levante
c.   Sevilla
d.   Barcelona

23.   As cunning as they were no one really thought the Foxes would win it, but they suprised the world of football when they won the English Premier League in 2016. What English football team is called the Foxes?
a.   Wolverhampton Wanderers
b.   Leicester City
c.   Oxford Town
d.   Port Vale

24.   Juventus, the name is very tempting to say again. This team bears very unusual nickname, what is the nickname?
a.   The Greater Pioneers
b.   The Juvenile Giraffes
c.   The Old Lady
d.   The Spring of Peace

25.   This German team is commonly regarded as 'Die Fohlen' (German for- the foals) in order save time that would have been spent pronouncing

the name in full and biting your tongue on the way (unless you are German). Which team is that?

a. Bayer Leverkusen
b. Borussia Dortmund
c. Borussia Monchengladbach
d. Bayern Munich

26.   On, BBC Radio 5, a pundit says that the Three Lions have a match at 7:45pm. Which country are you going to watch play on your TV, if you decide to watch the game?

a. Turkey
b. France
c. Netherlands
d. England

27.   The Belgian national football team shares its satanic nickname with a popular English football club. Which nickname?

a. The Red Devils
b. Practitioners of Law
c. The Political Dabblers
d. Satan

28.   This Italian club, also known as Giallorossi, has enjoyed a pretty good spell in Italian football, and also produced legendary striker, Francesco Totti. Their badge has the picture of two wolves suckling a bear. Which team is it?

a. AS Roma
b. AC Milan
c. Napoli
d. Internazionale Milan

29.   When a team gets battered by the Cityzens, which blue jersey English club won the game?

a. Manchester City
b. Brighton & Hove Albion
c. Leicester City
d. Birmingham City

30.   Which club, also known as the Rossoneri, is known for football legends like Maldini, Shevchenko, Seedorf and Ibrahimovich, to mention but a few, and also for their achievements in Italian and European football?

a. Genoa

b. Udinese

c. AC Milan

d. S.S.C Napoli

31. **Which British team became the first ever British team to win the European Cup?**

a. Man Utd

b. Celtic

c. Liverpool

d. Nottingham Forest

32. **Which of the following teams did Inter Milan not face on their journey to the 1967 European Cup Final?**

a. Vasas SC

b. CSKA Sofia

c. Sporting Club de Portugal

d. Real Madrid

33. **Which English team got into the final of the UEFA Cup 2 years in a row, failing to win both times?**

a. Birmingham

b. Dundee Utd

c. Liverpool

d. Leeds

34. **From 1968 to 1973, the UEFA Cup was won by an English club. But which of the following clubs was not one of the four English teams to win the Uefa Cup during that period of English domination?**

a. Wolves

b. Arsenal

c. Leeds

d. Tottenham

35. **Who was the first team ever to win the European Super Cup?**

a. Barcelona

b. Rangers

c. Ajax

d. HSV

36. **Who won the 1990-91 European Cup?**

a. Man Utd

b. Marseille

c. Red Star

d. Feyenoord

37.   **In what year did the Romanian side of Steaua Bucharest first win the European Cup?**

a. 1983-84
b. 1978-79
c. 1985-86
d. 1993-94

38.   **Who did PSV Eindhoven beat in the final of the 1987-88?**

a. Juventus
b. Barcelona
c. Benfica
d. Real Madrid

39.   **In the first 30 years of the UEFA Cup, which of the following teams won three cups?**

a. Parma
b. Ajax
c. Liverpool
d. Galatasaray

40.   **In 2002, Real Madrid won their _____ European Cup title.**

a. 19th
b. 3rd
c. 9th
d. 14th

41.   **The Old Firm refers to a what?**

a. A well respected groundsman at any club
b. Football ground
c. Derby
d. Sweeping attacking move

42.   **Which of the following Dutch clubs is the oldest?**

a. Sparta
b. Vitesse
c. Haarlem
d. Willem II

43.   **What is the common bond between Juventus, Bayern Munich, and Ajax?**

a. They all have always played in the top flight
b. They have won the most national titles in their respective countries
c. They all won the European Cup, the Cup Winners Cup and the UEFA Cup
d. They were founded on the same date

44.   Real Madrid won the first five editions of the European Cup, beating four different opponents. Who was their first victim?

a.   Stade Reims
b.   AC Milan
c.   Fiorentina
d.   Eintracht Frankfurt

45.   Which of these English clubs does not have a bird for a nickname?

a.   Newcastle United
b.   Sheffield Wednesday
c.   Manchester City
d.   Norwich City

46.   Once there were three different European club competitions. There was the European Cup for the champions, the UEFA Cup for the best few of the rest, and the European Cup winners cup. That competition merged with the UEFA Cup in 1999. Which club was the last one to win that competition?

a.   Chelsea
b.   VfB Stuttgart
c.   Real Mallorca
d.   Lazio Roma

47.   In 1963, the Bundesliga was formed. Which of the following was never relegated while playing 45 consecutive years in the German top flight?

a.   Werder Bremen
b.   Hamburger SV
c.   Bayern Munich
d.   VfB Stuttgart

48.   In 2008, the European Championships were held for the 13th time, hosted by Austria and Switzerland. Spain came out on top. What country was the outgoing champion?

a.   Czech Republic
b.   Greece
c.   The Netherlands
d.   Denmark

49.   Although football existed for quite a while already in England, a national competition only started in 1888, and 12 clubs participated. Which one of them came out on top in the first-ever Football League?

a.   Stoke

b. Notts County

c. Preston North End

d. Everton

50.   Football fans will remember the Munich air disaster in which almost a complete generation of promising youngsters from Manchester United was wiped out. Which other European club suffered the same fate some years before?

a. Valencia

b. Paris Saint German

c. Schalke 04

d. Torino

51.   How did Denmark qualify for (and then go on to win) the 1992 European Championship final?

a. By being elevated to the top of their qualifying group because Yugoslavia was disqualified when war broke out

b. Topping their qualify group on goal difference

c. By topping their qualifying group on the last day with a 3-0 win over Finland

d. Because they were the host nation

52.   Patrick Vieira is a French legend, but in which country was he born?

a. France

b. Ivory Coast

c. Senegal

d. Ghana

53.   Former Irish skipper Roy Keane was sent home from the 2002 World Cup finals tournament. Which other player was also sent home after having a falling out with the team's manager?

a. Mark Viduka

b. Zlakto Zahovic

c. Igor Tudor

d. Francesco Totti

54.   Before rising to fame as manager of Bolton Wanderers, which one of these teams did former England player Sam Allardyce manage for a short stint?

a. Boavista

b. Limerick City

c. Rapid Vienna

d. AZ Alkmar

55.   Which European club did Arsene Wenger manage before his stint with Grampus 8 in Japan?

a. Levante

b. Paris St Germain

c. Monaco

d. Rennes

56.   In the 1995 European Cup-Winners Cup final, Arsenal goal keeper David Seaman was lobbed from the halfway line by which player?

a. Zinidine Zidane

b. Nouridine Naybet

c. Luis Figo

d. Nayim

57.   In 2007, which player played in his fourth different Champions League with his 3rd different team?

a. Jurgen Klinsmann

b. David Platt

c. Franz Beckenbaur

d. Clarence Seedorf

58.   What happened at the 2002 World Cup finals tournament that had never happened before?

a. All the games were played under floodlights to suit central European TV stations

b. The previous winners (France) were knocked out in the first round

c. It took a penalty shoot out to decide the final

d. The Italians protested at the level of yellow cards being handed out

59.   In what year did the West Germany win its last major competition of the 20th century?

a. World Cup - Italy 1990

b. World Cup - Mexico 1986

c. European Championship - West Germany 1988

d. Confederations Cup - Saudi Arabia 1997

60.   Who did Olympique de Marseille defeat in the first-ever UEFA Champions league final in the 1992-93 season?

a. AC Milan

b. FC Porto

c. Ajax

d. Liverpool

61.   Who won Italy's Serie A for the 2019-20 season?

a. Lazio

b. Inter

c. Juventus

d. Atalanta

62.   France's Ligue 1 did not complete the season as Paris Saint-Germain was declared the league champion.

a. True
b. False

63.   Spain's La Liga saw Real Madrid win the league by how many points?

a. 3
b. 5
c. 7
d. 9

64.   The Bundesliga saw Bayern Munich win their _____ consecutive league title at the end of the 2019-2020 season.

a. eighth
b. fourth
c. second
d. sixth

65.   What club won Portugal's Primeira Liga?

a. Sporting
b. Benfica
c. Porto
d. Braga

66.   What team won the English Premier League?

a. Manchester City
b. Chelsea
c. Manchester United
d. Liverpool

67.   What team won Super League Greece at the end of the season?

a. Olympiacos
b. PAOK

68.   Turkey's Super Lig did not declare a champion.

c. True
d. False

69.   What team won the Russian Premier League?

a. Lokomotiv Moscow
b. Zenit Saint Petersburg
c. CSKA Moscow
d. Krasnodar

70.   What team won the Croatian First Football League?

a. Osijek
b. Lokomotiva

c. Dinamo Zagreb

d. Rijeka

71. Clubs such as Arsenal, Liverpool and Manchester United won loads of league titles in England during the 20th century, but which club, managed by Alf Ramsey, won their only title in season 1961-62?

a. Watford

b. Norwich City

c. Ipswich Town

d. Luton Town

72. The French title had a number of dominant clubs in the 20th century, such as Nantes, Saint Etienne and Marseille, but which club, managed by Gilbert Gress, won their only 20th century title in 1978-79?

a. Lille OSC

b. RC Strasbourg

c. OGC Nice

d. Girondins Bordeaux

73. Barcelona and Real Madrid, perhaps not surprisingly, won more than their fair share of Spanish titles during the 20th century, but which team, managed by Ramon Encinas, had a one-off success in 1945-46?

a. Espanyol

b. Real Zaragoza

c. Sevilla

d. Celta Vigo

74. Celtic and Rangers monopolised Scottish football in the 20th century, but occasionally another club would manage to break the duopoly. Which team, managed by Bob Shankly, won their only title of the century in 1961-62?

a. Motherwell

b. Kilmarnock

c. Third Lanark

d. Dundee

75. The top flight of Italian football in the 20th century saw the majority of titles won by Juventus, AC Milan or Inter Milan. Which team, managed by Manlio Scopigno, topped them all in 1969-70?

a. Parma

b. Venezia

c. Palermo

d. Cagliari

76.   Benfica, Sporting Lisbon and Porto won every Portuguese title bar one between them from 1935 until 2000. Which team, in 1945-46, were the only other team to get their hands on the silverware during this period?

a. Vitoria Setubal
b. Belenenses
c. Sporting Braga
d. Academica Coimbra

77.   The "big three" in Dutch football, after World War II, were Ajax, Feyenoord and PSV Eindhoven. Which team, managed by a German called Georg Kessler, were the surprise champions of 1980-81?

a. Sparta Rotterdam
b. Twente Enschede
c. AZ Alkmaar
d. Willem II

78.   The Greek title was dominated in the 20th century by Olympiacos, Panathinaikos and AEK Athens. Which team, managed by a Pole, Jacek Gmoch, were the surprise champions of 1987-88?

a. Larissa
b. Aris Salonika
c. PAOK Salonika
d. Panionios

79.   The top flight of Austria was dominated for many years after World War Two by the big Vienna clubs, FK Austria and Rapid, as well as Wacker Innsbruck. Which team, managed by Helmut Senekowitsch, won their only title in 1973-74?

a. VOEST Linz
b. Weiner SC
c. Admira
d. First Vienna

80.   The top league in Belgium has been dominated, since World War Two, by Anderlecht, Standard Liege and Club Brugge. Which team, managed by Felix Week, pulled off a solitary title victory in 1974-75?

a. RWD Molenbeek
b. Beerschot
c. Cercle Brugge
d. Union St Gilloise

81.   SK Sturm Graz plays for what country?

a. Czech Republic
b. Germany
c. Austria
d. Switzerland

82.   Boavista F.C. plays for which country?

a. Portugal
b. Italy
c. Spain
d. Malta

83.   In which country can AEK F.C. be found?

a. Sweden
b. Hungary
c. Russia
d. Greece

84.   In what country would you find Molde F.K.?

a. Iceland
b. Denmark
c. Norway
d. Sweden

85.   Parma A.C. plays in what country?

a. Spain
b. Greece
c. Portugal
d. Italy

86.   In which country would you find NK Maribor?

a. Belarus
b. Slovakia
c. Russia
d. Slovenia

87.   Deportivo La Coruna plays in which country?

a. Italy
b. Portugal
c. Spain
d. Andora

88.   S.C. Freiburg plays in which country?

a. Austria
b. Germany
c. Switzerland
d. France

89.   Grasshopper Club would be found playing in which country?
a.   Wales
b.   Switzerland
c.   England
d.   Republic of Ireland

90.   K.V. Mechelen plays in what country?
a.   France
b.   Netherlands
c.   Luxemburg
d.   Belgium

91.   What club has its team playing at the Santiago Bernabeu?
a.   Barcelona
b.   Valencia
c.   A.C Milan
d.   Real Madrid

92.   What are the traditional colors of Inter Milan?
a.   Red & White
b.   Red & Black
c.   Blue & Black
d.   Blue & White

93.   A player of which team was the top-scorer in Portugal in the 2001-02 season?
a.   Boavista
b.   Benfica
c.   Sporting
d.   F.C Porto

94.   What nationality were most of the imported players at Arsenal in the 2001-02 season?
a.   Dutch
b.   Italian
c.   French
d.   German

95.   Deportivo la Coruna is a small Spanish club who made big waves in Europe since 1990. How many times did the club win the title in Spain between 1990 and 2001?
a.   0
b.   3
c.   2
d.   1

96.   Have there ever been any transfers between the two rivals in Milan (A.C Milan and Inter)?

e. Yes
f. No

97.   For which Italian club did Zidane play?

a. Inter Milan
b. Juventus
c. A.C Milan
d. Lazio

98.   What club has the head of a greek hero on its crest?

a. Ajax Amsterdam
b. Bayern Munich
c. Panatinaikos Atena
d. P.S.G

99.   Which team lost two consecutive Champions League finals, in 2000 and 2001?

a. Valencia
b. Bayern Munich
c. Real Madrid
d. Manchester United

100.   What is the most famous football club in Birmingham?

a. Blackburn
b. Aston Villa
c. Tottenham
d. Everton

101.   Having helped the Soviet Union win the Gold Medal at the 1956 Melbourne Olympics, which wonderful talent failed to represent his nation at the 1958 World Cup, due to charges of rape?

a. Oleg Blokhin
b. Lev Yashin
c. Igor Netto
d. Eduard Streltsov

102.   Anatoly Banishevsky was responsible for an astonishing feat on his debut for the Soviet Union in 1965. What was it that he famously did?

a. He scored with a header from 40 yards out
b. He kissed all the Brazilian players on the lips at the start of the game
c. He started to juggle stones and dribble with the ball at the same time
d. He got sent off the field within 5 minutes of the kickoff

103. One of the greatest Bulgarian players ever had his life tragically cut short in 1971. Can you name this great player?
a. Dimitar Penev
b. Kiril Ivkov
c. Georgi Asparuhov
d. Hristo Bonev

104. Which of the following goalkeepers have earned the nickname, 'The man that stopped England', despite being referred to as a 'clown' by Brian Clough?
a. Boris Mikhailov
b. Rinat Dasayev
c. Jan Tomaszewki
d. Lev Yashin

105. In 2001, a man named Levan used a taxi to a hospital where he was training to be a doctor. When he left the taxi, three men bundled him into a car and a subsequent ransom demand for his release was made. Who was his famous footballing brother?
a. Temuri Ketsbaia
b. Georgi Kinkladze
c. Kakha Kaladze
d. Aleksandr Iashvili

106. The romance of football can direct one to scoring goals; many beautiful goals. Which of the following scored the most international goals in the 20th century?
a. Ferenc Puskas
b. Imre Schlosser
c. Sandor Kocsis
d. Lajos Tichy

107. Which Yugoslavian international scored the winning goal in a 1982 World Cup group game against Honduras?
a. Vladimir Petrovic
b. Nenad Stojkovic
c. Nikola Jovanovic
d. Dragan Pantelic

108. The uncle of Victor Piturca built a mausoleum which he slept in until his own death, for Victor's cousin, Florin.
a. True
b. False

109. **The home stadium of Dynamo Kiev was renamed after which famous former manager in 2002?**

a. Oleksiy Mykhaylichenko
b. Valeri Lobanovsky
c. Yozhef Sabo
d. Mykhailo Fomenko

110. **The romance of Eastern European football was extremely appreciated outside of Europe also. Against which International team did Pele play his final international game for Brazil against?**

a. Hungary
b. Yugoslavia
c. Czechoslovakia
d. Bulgaria

111. **Charlton Athletic are also known as the 'Addicks'. Who did they get this name from?**

a. Legendary player
b. Original chairman
c. Local chip shop owner
d. Original ground owner

112. **Who are the only non-league English club to win the FA Cup?**

a. Tottenham Hotspur
b. Preston North End
c. Manchester United
d. Stoke City

113. **The only non-league English club to win the FA Cup: when did this team achieve this feat?**

a. 1903
b. 1900
c. 1901
d. 1904

114. **What is the name of the official Czech Republic's international stadium?**

a. Tehelne Pole
b. Stadion Slaski
c. Vasil Levski
d. Stadion Evzen Rosicky

115. **What strange quirk did Daniel Passarella, former Argentina coach, have about picking his international squad?**

a. wouldn't pick players who played abroad

b. wouldn't pick players with drug problems

c. wouldn't pick players who were married

d. wouldn't pick players with long hair

116. Which number shirt would the Brazilian government like to retire, so that no Brazilian international would be allowed to wear?

a. 9

b. 10

c. 11

d. 4

117. Which famous English full-back was nicknamed 'Psycho' for his style of play?

a. Tony Adams

b. Ian Pearce

c. Sol Campbell

d. Stuart Pearce

118. What is the real name of the Brazilian legend, Pele?

a. Mauricio Alejandro Molina

b. Edson Arantes do Nascimento

c. Alejandro Dominguez

d. Daniel da Silva Carvalho

119. What was the score when England famously beat West Germany in the 1966 World Cup Final?

a. 1-0

b. 3-2

c. 2-1

d. 4-2

120. Which English football club was the first to win the domestic double in the 20th Century?

a. Tottenham Hotspur

b. Liverpool

c. Arsenal

d. Manchester United

121. Which club won the double the most times during the 20th century?

a. Tottenham Hotspur

b. Manchester United

c. Arsenal

d. Liverpool

122. Who was the first player over 50 years old to make an appearance for a top-flight English club?

a. Peter Shilton
b. Stanley Matthews
c. Neville Southall
d. Steve Ogrizovic

123.   What do Derby County blame any bad run of luck on?

a. Gypsy curse
b. John Whiteman's death
c. Ghost of Stan Goldman
d. Tottenham Hotspur

124.   What profession did legendary Welsh goalie Neville Southall have before making his league debut?

a. Electrician
b. Plumber
c. Teacher
d. Dustman

125.   In what year did Johann Cruyff make his league debut for Dutch giants, Ajax?

a. 1963
b. 1967
c. 1965
d. 1964

126.   What was the score of the 1958 FA Cup Final?

a. 2-0
b. 3-1
c. 2-1
d. 3-0

127.   Machester United were the losers the 1958 FA Cup Final. Who were the winners?

a. Wolverhampton Wanderers
b. Aston Villa
c. Tottenham Hotspur
d. Bolton Wanderers

128.   How many caps did England's longest serving goalkeeper, Peter Shilton, achieve?

a. 125
b. 106
c. 98
d. 137

129.   When ex-England and Spurs centre back, Gary Mabbutt, was mugged in July 2001 he was, above all else, distressed by the loss of which item?

a. Credit cards
b. FA cup winner's medal
c. Photo of his wife
d. Rolex watch

130.   Who was the original footballing SAS?

a. Shearer and Sheringham
b. Shearer and Scholes
c. Sheringham and Sutton
d. Shearer and Sutton

131.   Who sponsored Italian club AC Milan?

a. JJB Sports
b. Carlsberg
c. Bwin
d. tomtom

132.   Which of the following did EBB sponsor?

a. Barrow
b. Charlton Athletic
c. Wolfsburg
d. Aldershot Town

133.   Who sponsored Italian club Lazio?

a. Nobody
b. Mini
c. AOL
d. Pixer

134.   Which of the following sponsored French club Lyon?

a. None of these
b. Novotel
c. HSBC
d. Microsoft

135.   This sponsor is an Australian based company. They supply electrical supplies and was founded by Chinese. Which company is this that sponsored Sydney FC?

a. Bing Lee
b. AIG
c. Air France
d. Impact

136.   Who sponsored the American club LA Galaxy?

a. Bizjournals

b. Game

c. AE

d. Herbalife

137.   Which car sponsored Spanish club Atletico Madrid?

a. Honda

b. Ford

c. Kia

d. BMW

138.   Who was the sponsor of Greek club AEK Athens?

a. Samsung

b. Eurostar

c. Sky Sports

d. LG

139.   Who are English club Bolton sponsored by?

a. Nike

b. Adidas

c. Puma

d. Reebok

140.   Name the team that is sponsored by Intersports?

a. Fulham

b. Real Madrid

c. Portsmouth

d. None of these

141.   In which country does Anderlecht play?

a. Denmark

b. Switzerland

c. Germany

d. Belgium

142.   Atalanta plays in which country?

a. Turkey

b. Italy

c. Spain

d. France

143.   Airdrieonians are from which country?

a. Scotland

b. Finland

c. Romania

d. Malta

144.   Auxerre come from which country?

a. France

b. Portugal

c. Macedonia

d. Lithuania

145.   Alaves is a club which plays in which country?

a. Greece

b. Spain

c. Portugal

d. Croatia

146.   AIK Solna come from which country?

a. Spain

b. Slovakia

c. Sweden

d. Switzerland

147.   What country does the team Angers play in?

a. Estonia

b. France

c. Norway

d. Bulgaria

148.   AA Gent come from which country?

a. Luxembourg

b. Austria

c. Hungary

d. Belgium

149.   AZ Alkmaar lost to Ipswich Town in the 1981 UEFA Cup Final. What country are they from?

a. Denmark

b. Poland

c. Slovenia

d. Holland

150.   Aarhus GF come from which country?

a. Germany

b. Denmark

c. Belgium

d. Austria

151.   Alverca plays in which country?

a. Albania

b. Portugal

c. Greece

d. Spain

152.   Ankaragucu come from which country?

a. Armenia

b. Cyprus

c. Turkey

d. Belarus

153.   The team Ararat Yerevan plays in which country?

a. Albania

b. Georgia

c. Ukraine

d. Armenia

154.   Amica Wronki come from which country?

a. Austria

b. Bulgaria

c. Poland

d. Russia

155.   Alania Vladikavkaz come from which country?

a. Poland

b. Macedonia

c. Ukraine

d. Russia

156.   In 1996-97, Brazilian Ronaldo won it by scoring 34 goals for which team?

a. Real Madrid

b. PSV Eindhoven

c. Barcelona

d. Inter Milan

157.   In 1998-99, Mario Jardel won the award playing for FC Porto. How many goals did he end the season with?

a. 38

b. 28

c. 36

d. 33

158.   In 1999-2000, the award was won with 30 goals by which Premier League player?

a. Alan Shearer

b. Kevin Phillips

c.   Dwight Yorke

d.   Andy Cole

159.   In 2000-01, the award was won with 35 goals by which player?

a.   Luis Figo

b.   Ruud Van Nistelrooy

c.   Henrik Larsson

d.   David Trezeguet

160.   In 2002-03, the award went to Roy Makaay with 29 goals. But for which club was he playing?

a.   Tenerife

b.   Feyenoord

c.   Deportivo

d.   Bayern Munich

161.   In 2003-04, Thierry Henry of Arsenal won the Golden Boot. How many goals did he score?

a.   24

b.   30

c.   28

d.   26

162.   In 2004-05, the award had to be split between 2 players who each scored 25 goals for their respective clubs. Thierry Henry was again one, but who was the other?

a.   Adriano

b.   Ruud Van Nistelrooy

c.   Andriy Shevchenko

d.   Diego Forlan

163.   In 2005-06, 31 goals was enough to win the award. Which Serie A player won it?

a.   David Trezeguet

b.   Andriy Shevchenko

c.   Christiano Lucarelii

d.   Luca Toni

164.   In 2006-07, which World Cup winner won the Golden Boot by scoring 26 goals for his club?

a.   Luca Toni

b.   Thierry Henry

c.   Ronaldinho

d.   Francesco Totti

165.   In 2007-08, Cristiano Ronaldo of Manchester United won the Golden
Boot. How many goals did the midfielder score in that season?
a. 29
b. 31
c. 30
d. 32

166.   What were 'The Golden Team' known as in Hungarian?
a. Aranycsillag
b. Aranycsapat
c. Aranycsap
d. Aranycsempe

167.   Who was the coach of 'The Golden Team'?
a. Gusztáv Sebes
b. Gábor Juhász
c. Gyúla Szakács
d. György Zigány

168.   At the 1952 Olympics in Helsinki, 'The Golden Team' won the final
and the gold medal against Yugoslavia. What was the final score?
a. 1 - 0
b. 3 - 2
c. 2 - 1
d. 2 - 0

169.   In 1953, Hungary became the first non-British team to defeat
England on their own home soil in an invitational played at Wembley on
November 25th. What was the score?
a. 2 - 0
b. 6 - 3
c. 3 - 1
d. 4 - 2

170.   Which of the players scored 84 goals in 85 international matches
for Hungary, and in 1995 was recognized as the 20th Century's top
scorer by the International Federation of Football History and Statistics?
a. Ferenc Puskas
b. Jenö Buzanszky
c. Gyula Grosics
d. Nandor Hidegkuti

171.   Hungary set a record for the largest unbeaten sequence at
international level for how many consecutive wins?
a. 32

b. 30

c. 24

d. 21

172.   From 15 June 1952 until 18 February 1956, and excepting the 1954 World Cup, how many victories did 'The Golden Team' amass?

a. 29

b. 36

c. 43

d. 31

173.   Hungary set a record for the highest ever ELO football rating of how many points, posted in June 1954?

a. 2116pts

b. 2173 pts

c. 2128pts

d. 2135pts

174.   Which of the team opened a restaurant in Barcelona, Spain, after retirement called 'Tete D'Or'?

a. József Bozsik

b. Ferenc Puskás

c. Sándor Kocsis

d. Zoltán Czibor

175.   What was the reason 'The Golden Team' disbanded, never to play together again?

a. Retirements

b. 1956 Suez Crisis

c. 1956 Hungarian Uprising

d. World War II

Answers Round One

1. Juventus
2. Ruud Gullit
3. Bologna
4. Yes
5. Italy
6. Eintracht Frankfurt
7. Monaco
8. Penalty shootout
9. Villareal
10. Greece
11. Manchester United
12. Turkey
13. Argentina
14. Amsterdam
15. Germany
16. 4
17. 0
18. Glasgow
19. Ireland
20. Real Madrid
21. Arsenal
22. Barcelona
23. Leicester City
24. The Old Lady
25. Borussia Monchengladbach
26. England
27. The Red Devils
28. AS Roma
29. Manchester City
30. AC Milan
31. Celtic
32. Sporting Club de Portugal
33. Birmingham
34. Wolves
35. Ajax
36. Red Star
37. 1985-86
38. Benfica
39. Liverpool
40. 9th
41. Derby
42. Sparta
43. They all won the European Cup, the Cup Winners Cup and the UEFA Cup
44. Stade Reims
45. Manchester City
46. Lazio Roma
47. Hamburger SV
48. Greece
49. Preston North End
50. Torino
51. By being elevated to the top of their qualifying group because

Yugoslavia was disqualified when war broke out

52. Senegal

53. Zlakto Zahovic

54. Limerick City

55. Monaco

56. Nayim

57. Clarence Seedorf

58. The previous winners (France) were knocked out in the first round

59. World Cup - Italy 1990

60. AC Milan

61. Juventus

62. True

63. 5

64. eighth

65. Porto

66. Liverpool

67. Olympiacos

68. False

69. Zenit Saint Petersburg

70. Dinamo Zagreb

71. Ipswich Town

72. RC Strasbourg

73. Sevilla

74. Dundee

75. Cagliari

76. Belenenses

77. AZ Alkmaar

78. Larissa

79. VOEST Linz

80. RWD Molenbeek

81. Austria

82. Portugal

83. Greece

84. Norway

85. Italy

86. Slovenia

87. Spain

88. Germany

89. Switzerland

90. Belgium

91. Real Madrid

92. Blue & Black

93. Sporting

94. French

95. 1

96. Yes

97. Juventus

98. Ajax Amsterdam

99. Valencia

100. Aston Villa

101. Eduard Streltsov

102. He scored with a header from 40 yards out

103. Georgi Asparuhov

104. Jan Tomaszewki

105.	Kakha Kaladze	132.	Aldershot Town
106.	Ferenc Puskas	133.	Nobody
107.	Vladimir Petrovic	134.	Novotel
108.	true	135.	Bing Lee
109.	Valeri Lobanovsky	136.	Herbalife
110.	Yugoslavia	137.	Kia
111.	Local chip shop owner	138.	LG
112.	Tottenham Hotspur	139.	Reebok
113.	1901	140.	None of these
114.	Stadion Evzen Rosicky	141.	Belgium
115.	wouldn't pick players with long hair	142.	Italy
		143.	Scotland
116.	10	144.	France
117.	Stuart Pearce	145.	Spain
118.	Edson Arantes do Nascimento	146.	Sweden
		147.	France
119.	4-2	148.	Belgium
120.	Tottenham Hotspur	149.	Holland
121.	Manchester United	150.	Denmark
122.	Stanley Matthews	151.	Portugal
123.	Gypsy curse	152.	Turkey
124.	Dustman	153.	Armenia
125.	1965	154.	Poland
126.	2-0	155.	Russia
127.	Bolton Wanderers	156.	Barcelona
128.	125	157.	36
129.	Rolex watch	158.	Kevin Phillips
130.	Shearer and Sutton	159.	Henrik Larsson
131.	Bwin	160.	Deportivo

161.	30		169.	6 - 3
162.	Diego Forlan		170.	Ferenc Puskas
163.	Luca Toni		171.	32
164.	Francesco Totti		172.	43
165.	31		173.	2173 pts
166.	Aranycsapat		174.	Sándor Kocsis
167.	Gusztáv Sebes		175.	1956 Hungarian Uprising
168.	2 - 0			

Round 2 : Football Players Trivia

1. Sporting Lisbon - Barcelona - Real Madrid?
a. Rivaldo
b. Rui Costa
c. Hernan Crespo
d. Luis Figo

2. FC Koln - Rapid Vienna - Bayern Munich - Udinese?
a. Dietmar Hamann
b. Abede Pele
c. Carsten Jancker
d. Sami Kuffour

3. Paris Saint Germain - Arsenal - Real Madrid - Paris Saint Germain - Liverpool (Loan)- Manchester City?
a. Patrik Berger
b. Nicolas Anelka
c. John Arne Riise
d. Jari Litmanen

4. Dinamo Kiev - AC Milan?
a. Andriy Shevchenko
b. Andrei Kanchelskis
c. Hernan Crespo
d. Victor Onopko

5. Leeds United - Peterborough United - Birmingham City - Queens Park Rangers - Arsenal - Manchester City?
a. Lee Dixon

b. David Seaman

c. Nigel Winterburn

d. Richard Wright

6. Castellon - Valencia - Valencia 'B' - Valencia - Lazio - Barcelona (Loan) - Middlesbrough (Loan)?

a. Gaizka Mendieta

b. Fabio Cannavaro

c. Fernando Hierro

d. John Carew

7. University de Chile - River Plate - Lazio - Juventus?

a. Diego Forlan

b. Mirandinha

c. Martin Palermo

d. Marcelo Salas

8. Watford - Liverpool - Aston Villa - West Ham United - Manchester City?

a. David James

b. Steve Staunton

c. Trevor Sinclair

d. Gary Walsh

9. Fortuna Dusseldorf - SV Hamburg - Glasgow Rangers - SV Hamburg?

a. Andreas Brehme

b. Marco Negri

c. Jorg Albertz

d. Phil Masinga

10.   RBC Roosendaal - NAC - Glasgow Celtic - Nottingham Forest - Vitesse Arnhem - Benfica - Feyenoord?

a. Pierre van Hooijdonk

b. Berry van Aerle

c. Henrik Larsson

d. Brian Laudrup

11.   Lazio - Ternana - Lazio - Juventus - Napoli - Juventus - AC Milan - Glasgow Celtic - Sheffield Wednesday - West Ham United - Charlton Athletic?

a. Roberto Di Matteo

b. Juninho

c. Pierluigi Casiraghi

d. Paolo Di Canio

12.   Perugia - Avellino - Casertana - Avellino - Reggiana - Juventus - Middlesbrough - Marseilles - Lazio - Derby County?

a. Mirandinha

b. Fabrizio Ravanelli

c. Christian Abbiati

d. Robeto Mancini

13.   Hyeres - Meaux - Laval - Strasbourg - Chelsea - Marseilles?

a. Frank LeBoeuf

b. Marcel Desailly

c. Laurent Blanc

d. Emerson Thome

14.   Den Bosch - Heerenveen - PSV Eindhoven - Manchester United?

a. Ruud van Nistelrooy

b. Jaap Stam

c. Ronny Johnsen

d. Raimond van der Gouw

15.   Ajax Amsterdam - FC Twente - Ajax Amsterdam - Barcelona - Glasgow Rangers?

a. Bert Konterman

b. Frank de Boer

c. Ronald de Boer

d. Marc Overmars

16.   Borussia Monchenglanbach - Bayern Munich - Fiorentina - Borussia Monchengladbach - Bayern Munich - Wolfsburg?

a. Alexander Zickler

b. Stefan Effenberg

c. Michael Tarnat

d. Mehmet Scholl

17.   Budocnost - Partizan Belgrade - Valencia - Real Madrid - Fiorentina- Levante?

a. Gabriel Batistuta

b. Enrico Chiesa

c. Nuno Gomes

d. Predrag Mijatovic

18.   Ermis Amyuntaiou - Pontoi Veroias - Olympiakos - Newcastle United?

a. Nikos Dabizas

b. Shola Ameobi

c. Marcelino

d. Lormano Lua-Lua

19.	Arsenal - Bradford City (Loan) - Arsenal - Middlesbrough - Aston Villa - Portsmouth?

a.	Dion Dublin
b.	Lee Hendrie
c.	Paul Merson
d.	Ian Taylor

20.	Leeds United - Oldham Athletic - Manchester United - Wolverhampton Wanderers?

a.	Joe Jordan
b.	Eric Cantona
c.	Johnny Giles
d.	Denis Irwin

21.	Ceske Budejovice - Viktoria Zizkov - Slavia Prague - Manchester United - Benfica - Lazio - Sparta Prague?

a.	Jaap Stam
b.	Karel Poborsky
c.	Claudio Lopez
d.	Dejan Stankovic

22.	Sporting Lisbon - West Ham United (Loan) - Ajax Amsterdam - Benfica - Atletico Madrid?

a.	Ivan Amaya
b.	Santi
c.	Dani
d.	Toni

23.	St. Mirren - Motherwell - Borussia Dortmund - Glasgow Celtic?

a.	Paul McStay
b.	Jackie McNamara
c.	Owen Hargreaves
d.	Paul Lambert

24.	Manchester United - Aston Villa - Manchester United - Chelsea?

a.	Dwight Yorke
b.	Mark Bosnich
c.	Mark Robins
d.	Dion Dublin

25.	Manchester United - Barcelona - Bayern Munich (Loan) - Manchester United - Chelsea - Southampton - Everton - Blackburn Rovers?

a.	Henning Berg
b.	Keith Gillespie

c. John Curtis

d. Mark Hughes

26.   **What's the first name of Zidane the former French international player?**

a. Zizou

b. Zinezine

c. Zizu

d. Zinedine

27.   **What's the first name of Mendieta the former Lazio and Spain player?**

a. Gaizka

b. Gazka

c. Kaizka

d. Kazka

28.   **What's the first name of the former Italian player Del Piero?**

a. Paolo

b. Gianni

c. Filippo

d. Alessandro

29.   **What's the first name of the retired Czech player Nedved?**

a. Karel

b. Pavel

c. Andre

d. Kaziri

30.   **What's the first name of the former Manchester United player Beckham?**

a. David

b. John

c. Paul

d. Robbie

31.   **What's the first name of Shevchenko the former AC Milan player?**

a. Ashkiri

b. Andriy

c. Andriti

d. Ahmed

32.   **What is the first name of the retired Italian player Zola?**

a. Marco

b. Simone

c. Paolo

d. Gianfranco

33. **What's the first name of one of the most exciting players the late 1990s and early 2000s - Figo?**

a. Manoel
b. Luis
c. Pablo
d. Jorge

34. **What's the first name of the former Norwegian and Valencia player Carew?**

a. John
b. Jahn
c. Jon
d. Jan

35. **What's the first name of the former captain of Bayern Munich, Effenberg?**

a. Oliver
b. Mehmet
c. Stefan
d. Franz

36. **What's the first name of the retired Swedish international player Osmanovski?**

a. Yksel
b. Yiksel
c. Myklas
d. Iskel

37. **What's the first name of the retired Trinidad and Tobago player Yorke?**

a. James
b. Dylon
c. Gregor
d. Dwight

38. **What's the first name of the Australian born player Aloisi?**

a. Paul
b. Stephen
c. Martin
d. John

39. **What's the first name of the Japanese player Nakata?**

a. Hidetoshi
b. Sagama

c. Hidaka

d. Hiriuka

40.   **What's the first name of Veron?**

a. Juan Sebastian

b. Andre Juan

c. Juan Andre

d. Cristiano Juan

41.   **What's the first name of the Argentinian striker Batistuta?**

a. Claudio

b. Diego

c. Celso

d. Gabriel

42.   **What's the first name of the African player Mboma?**

a. Paul

b. Partiri

c. Peter

d. Patrick

43.   **What are the first names of the retired Norwegian player Solskjaer?**

a. Adam Claude

b. Tore Andre

c. Ole Gunnar

d. Adam Paul

44.   **What's the first name of the retired Australian striker Viduka?**

a. John

b. Fabian

c. Peter

d. Mark

45.   **What's the first name of the Romanian international Petrescu?**

a. Dan

b. Mark

c. Jan

d. Sandi

46.   **What's the first name of the talented Croatian player Boban?**

a. Zvoren

b. Zvone

c. Zvonimir

d. Zvominir

47.   **What's the first name of the Milan player Seedorf?**

a. Clarence
b. Floyd
c. Patrick
d. Mark

48.   What's the first name of the player Owen?
a. David
b. Michael
c. Matthew
d. Paul

49.   What's the first name of the retired Turkish international Sukur?
a. Musmeth
b. Ahmed
c. Hakan
d. Fatih

50.   What's the first name of the Birkirkara player Nwoko?
a. Afkiri
b. Ameni
c. Tijani
d. Chucks

51.   Where are Ronaldo and Messi from?
a. Both are from Spain
b. Brazil and Italy
c. Portugal and Argentina
d. Both are from Italy

52.   Cristiano Ronaldo joined Real Madrid at the beginning of the 2009-10 season.
a. True
b. False

53.   Both Messi and Ronaldo have won the FIFA World Player of the Year. Did Messi win it before Ronaldo?
c. Yes
d. No

54.   Was Lionel Messi the first to break the 50 goals mark in the La Liga, the Spanish first division?
e. Yes
f. No

55.   At which club did Cristiano Ronaldo start his professional career?
a. Manchester United
b. Flamengo

c. Indepeniente

d. Sporting Lisbon

56.   How many goals did Lionel Messi score in his first full season in the Barcelona first team?

a. 21

b. 2

c. 8

d. 16

57.   Between 2008 and 2012 Ronaldo and Messi have won 4 European Golden Shoe awards. Who was the other player to win this title in those years?

a. Wayne Rooney

b. Didier Drogba

c. Radomel Falcao

d. Diego Forlán

58.   Between 2008 and 2012 Messi and Ronaldo won all the FIFA World Player of the Year awards. In 2007 another player won. Who was he?

a. Didier Drogba

b. Xavi

c. Iniesta

d. Kaka

59.   How does Messi score most of his goals?

a. Heel

b. Right foot

c. Left foot

d. Header

60.   How does Cristiano Ronaldo score most of his goals?

a. Left foot

b. Heel

c. Right foot

d. Header

61.   Which is the club where Brazilian striker Pele became an idol?

a. Palmeiras.

b. Santos.

c. Sao Paulo.

d. Corinthians.

62.   Which is the Italian club where striker Marco Van Basten became an idol?

a. Juventus.

b. Lazio.

c. Inter.

d. AC Milan.

63.   Which are the clubs where striker Johan Cruyff became an idol?

a. Ajax, PSV Eindhoven.

b. Ajax, Real Madrid.

c. Barcelona, Inter.

d. Ajax, Barcelona.

64.   Which is the club where striker Gerd Muller became an idol?

a. Bayern Munchen.

b. Borussia Dortmund.

c. Hamburg SV.

d. Kaiserslautern.

65.   Which is the club where Argentinian player Diego Armando Maradona became an idol?

a. Real Madrid.

b. Napoli.

c. Sampdoria.

d. River Plate.

66.   Which is the club where Kenny Dalglish became an idol?

a. Liverpool.

b. West Ham United.

c. Everton.

d. Manchester United.

67.   Which is the club where French player Zinedine Zidane is really an idol?

a. Paris Saint Germain.

b. Juventus.

c. Roma.

d. Parma.

68.   Which is the club where Uruguayan player Enzo Francescoli became an idol?

a. Boca Juniors.

b. Flamengo.

c. Valencia C.F.

d. River Plate.

69.   Which is the club where Bulgarian player Hristo Stoichkov became an idol?

a. Real Madrid.

b. Inter.

c. Milan A.C.

d. F.C.Barcelona.

70. **Which is the club where Bobby Charlton became an idol?**

a. Liverpool.

b. Tottenham Hotspur

c. Arsenal.

d. Manchester United.

71. **Which are the clubs where Portuguese player Paolo Futre became an idol?**

a. Oporto, Real Madrid.

b. Benfica, Atletico Madrid.

c. Porto, Atletico Madrid.

d. Sporting Lisbon, Athletic Bilbao.

72. **Which is the club where Italian goalkeeper Dino Zoff became an idol?**

a. Genoa.

b. Fiorentina.

c. Juventus.

d. Torino.

73. **Which is the club where defender Franco Baresi became an idol?**

a. Milan A.C.

b. Fiorentina.

c. Inter.

d. Lazio S.S.

74. **Which are the clubs where Luis Suarez became an idol?**

a. Valencia and Inter

b. Lazio and Benfica

c. Barcelona and Juventus

d. Liverpool and Barcelona

75. **Which is the club where striker Ally McCoist became an idol?**

a. Rangers Glasgow.

b. Aberdeen.

c. Celtic Glasgow.

d. Dundee United.

Answers Round 2

1. Luis Figo
2. Carsten Jancker
3. Nicolas Anelka
4. Andriy Shevchenko
5. David Seaman
6. Gaizka Mendieta
7. Marcelo Salas
8. David James
9. Jorg Albertz
10. Pierre van Hooijdonk
11. Paolo Di Canio
12. Fabrizio Ravanelli
13. Frank LeBoeuf
14. Ruud van Nistelrooy
15. Ronald de Boer
16. Stefan Effenberg
17. Predrag Mijatovic
18. Nikos Dabizas
19. Paul Merson
20. Denis Irwin
21. Karel Poborsky
22. Dani
23. Paul Lambert
24. Mark Bosnich
25. Mark Hughes
26. Zinedine
27. Gaizka
28. Alessandro
29. Pavel
30. David
31. Andriy
32. Gianfranco
33. Luis
34. John
35. Stefan
36. Yksel
37. Dwight
38. John
39. Hidetoshi
40. Juan Sebastian
41. Gabriel
42. Patrick
43. Ole Gunnar
44. Mark
45. Dan
46. Zvonimir
47. Clarence
48. Michael
49. Hakan
50. Chucks
51. Portugal and Argentina
52. True
53. No
54. Yes
55. Sporting Lisbon
56. 8

57. Diego Forlán

58. Kaka

59. Left foot

60. Right foot

61. Santos.

62. AC Milan.

63. Ajax, Barcelona.

64. Bayern Munchen.

65. Napoli.

66. Liverpool.

67. Juventus.

68. River Plate.

69. F.C.Barcelona.

70. Manchester United.

71. Porto, Atletico Madrid.

72. Juventus.

73. Milan A.C.

74. Liverpool and Barcelona

75. Rangers Glasgow.

Round 3: History of the World Cup Trivia

1. Italy won the 1938 World Cup, but which country was the runners up?
a.   Brazil
b.   Hungary
c.   Sweden
d.   France

2. Which country won the 1962 World Cup?
a.   Czechoslovakia
b.   Yugoslavia
c.   Chile
d.   Brazil

3. In 1990, West Germany won the World Cup. Who was the German manager?
a.   Franz Beckenbauer
b.   Sepp Herberger
c.   Helmut Schoen
d.   Berti Vogts

4. Which French footballer scored twice in the 1998 World Cup final?
a.   Emmanuel Petit
b.   Marcel Desailly
c.   Patrick Vieira
d.   Zinedine Zidane

5. Which team won the World Cup in 1954?

a. Hungary
b. U.S.A
c. Scotland
d. West Germany

6. In the 1994 final between Brazil and Italy, the Cup was won by which method?

a. Team that had more corners
b. Extra-Time
c. Penalties
d. Golden goal

7. Who did Argentina beat in the final of the World Cup in 1978?

a. Italy
b. Germany
c. Netherlands
d. Scotland

8. What was the attendance at the Romania v Peru match in the 1930 World Cup in Uruguay?

a. 700
b. 1500
c. 1000
d. 300

9. Who scored against France in 27 seconds in the 1982 World Cup?

a. Bryan Robson
b. Trevor Brooking
c. Kevin Keegan
d. Glenn Hoddle

10.   In what year were substitutes used for the first time in the World Cup?

a. 1958
b. 1966
c. 1970
d. 1982

11.   How many national teams played in the qualification games for the first World Cup in 1930?

a. 13
b. 47
c. 21
d. There were no qualification games

12.   In what place did the United States finish in the 1930 World Cup in Uruguay?

a.   2nd
b.   3rd
c.   4th
d.   5th

13.   Who won the 1938 World Cup?

a.   Brazil
b.   France
c.   Italy
d.   Uruguay

14.   There was no Final in the 1950 World Cup?

a.   True
b.   False

15.   Where was the 1954 World Cup final played?

a.   Basel Stadium
b.   Olympiastadion
c.   Wankdorf Stadium
d.   Grashoppers Stadium

16.   In the finals of 1954 in Switzerland, Germany defeated Hungary 3-2. Both teams had already played against each other earlier during this World Cup. What was the score in this game?

a.   Hungary 7 Germany 0
b.   Hungary 5 Germany 1
c.   Hungary 8 Germany 3
d.   Hungary 9 Germany 2

17.   Which team finished in second place in the 1958 World Cup in Sweden?

a.   Brazil
b.   Sweden
c.   Germany
d.   Italy

18.   The first World Cup was a cup that should be kept by the team that would win it three times, which Brazil achieved in 1970. Brazil's second victory in the championships was 1962 in Chile. What was the name of this famous Cup?

a.   FIFA World Cup
b.   Golden World Cup
c.   Jules Rimet Cup

d.   Otto Nerz Cup

19.   **Who was the line referee in the World Cup final of 1966 in England between England and Germany who told the referee that he considered the famous Wembley goal a valid one?**

a.   Tofik Bachramov

b.   John Finney

c.   Gottfried Dienst

d.   Juergen Kreitlein

20.   **Mexico 1970: which game of this World Cup tournament is considered by many historians to have been the most exciting game in World Cup history?**

a.   Italy v Germany

b.   Brazil v Uruguay

c.   Brazil v Italy

d.   Uruguay v Germany

21.   **West Germany 1974: who scored Holland's goal against Germany in the final?**

a.   Johan Neeskens

b.   Johan Cruyff

c.   Willy Van De Kerkhof

d.   Van Ierssel

22.   **What did the 1974 tournament in West Germany have in common with the 1978 finals in Argentina?**

a.   Zaire did not participate in both tournaments

b.   Holland lost in the final in both tournaments

c.   Austria played in both tournaments

d.   In both tournaments less than 3 own goals were scored

23.   **Who was Germany's goalkeeper in the semi finals of 1982 in Spain, who knocked out France's Patrick Battiston?**

a.   Eike Immel

b.   Uli Stein

c.   Harald Schumacher

d.   Sepp Maier

24.   **What did Diego Maradona call the infamous handball goal in the 1986 quarter final game against England?**

a.   The Hand of God

b.   The Fingers of Pain

c.   The Fist of Pleasure

d.   The Thumbs of Jesus

25.   Italy 1990: who scored the winning goal in the final for Germany in the 85th minute?

a.   Andreas Brehme

b.   Juergen Klinsmann

c.   Lothar Matthaeus

d.   Thomas Haessler

26.   Who shot the last penalty for Italy over the crossbar in the final against Brazil at World Cup 1994 in the United States?

a.   Mauro Tassotti

b.   Roberto Baggio

c.   Claudio Caniggia

d.   Gianluca Pagliuca

27.   Who scored the first 'Golden Goal' of World Cup history in the 1998 World Cup tournament in France?

a.   Zinedine Zidane

b.   Christophe Dugarry

c.   Emmanuel Petit

d.   Laurent Blanc

28.   How many teams won all of their 3 group games in World Cup 2002 in Japan/South Korea?

a.   3

b.   2

c.   6

d.   5

29.   Which of these players have scored the most goals in one single World Cup tournament?

a.   Just Fontaine

b.   Pele

c.   Gerd Mueller

d.   Ferenc Puskas

30.   What famous Football player's real name is Edson Arantes do Nascimento?

a.   Jairzinho

b.   Pele

c.   Eusebio

d.   Ronaldo

31.   Which of the following teams did not win the World Cup when it hosted the tournament?

a.   England

b. Brazil

c. Germany

d. Argentina

32.   **Where was the first game of the World Cup 2002 played?**

a. Sapporo

b. Seoul

c. Yokohama

d. Ibaraki

33.   **Which of these players scored more World Cup goals?**

a. Gerd Muller

b. Just Fontaine

c. Pele

d. Diego Maradona

34.   **There were many surprises linked to the World Cup tournament 2002 in Japan and South Korea. Many good teams did not make it very far. Which of these didn't even qualify?**

a. England

b. Argentina

c. Holland

d. France

35.   **Which country was the first to win two World Cups?**

a. Germany

b. Uruguay

c. Italy

d. Brazil

36.   **Perhaps the greatest 'left foot' in the history of the Italian football: who was acknowledged as the star and hero of the Italian squad during the 1970 World Cup held in Mexico?**

a. Gigi Riva

b. Giuseppe Meazza

c. Paolo Rossi

d. Fabio Capello

37.   **Thirteen national teams finally participated in the 1950 World Cup held in Brazil, although sixteen had qualified for this tournament. Which three failed to appear?**

a. West Germany , Austria and China

b. Honduras , Israel and North Korea

c. Mongolia , Portugal and Norway

d. India , Scotland and Turkey

38. **Who was the first player to score a hat-trick in a World Cup final?**

a. Geoff Hurst for England (against West Germany in 1966).

b. Mario Kempes for Argentina (against the Netherlands in 1978).

c. Pele for Brazil (against Sweden in 1958).

d. Paolo Rossi for Italy (against West Germany in 1982).

39. **Who scored the winning goal for Germany against Argentina in the 1990 World Cup final held in Italy?**

a. Pier Littbarski

b. Lothar Matthaeus

c. Andreas Brehme

d. Rudi Voeller

40. **There is only one World Cup Final in the history of the sport, in which the team that eventually lost the match and consequently the trophy were leading at half-time. Do you remember which Final this was?**

a. Uruguay v Argentina 4 - 2 (1930 Tournament)

b. Brazil v Czechoslovakia 3 - 1 (1962 Tournament)

c. West Germany v Hungary 3 - 2 (1954 Tournament)

d. West Germany v Netherlands 2 - 1 (1974 Tournament)

41. **What is the largest defeat that West Germany has experienced during a World Cup tournament?**

a. 1-3

b. 0-3

c. 3-8

d. 3-6

42. **How many goals did French star Zinedine Zidane score during the 1998 tournament, held in France?**

a. 6

b. 7

c. 5

d. 2

43. **What was the trophy's name up to the 1970 tournament held in Mexico?**

a. Stanley Mathews

b. Jacques Cousteau

c. Jules Rimet

d. Winston Churchhill

44. **Who scored The Netherlands' only goal in the final of 1978 tournament?**

a. Dirk Nanninga

b.   Rob Rensenbrink

c.   Johnny Rep

d.   Ari Haan

45.   **After Pele suffered a serious injury during the 1962 tournament in Chile, who was the player that replaced him in the Brazilian starting squad?**

a.   Tostao

b.   Zizinho

c.   Rivelino

d.   Amarildo

46.   **Which players produced The Netherlands' two goals in the unforgettable win against Brazil in the 1974 tournament?**

a.   Rep and Neeskens

b.   Neeskens and Cruijff

c.   Krol and Rensenbrink

d.   Cruijff and van Hanegem

47.   **Who was the coach of the Italian winning squads of 1934 and 1938?**

a.   Vittorio Pozzo

b.   Eugenio Vicini

c.   Enzo Bearzot

d.   Fabio Valcareggi

48.   **How many World Cup tournaments did Argentinian Mario Kempes participate in?**

a.   2

b.   4

c.   1

d.   3

49.   **Who was the first player in the World Cup history that has scored five goals in one single match?**

a.   Russian Oleg Salenko against Cameroon in USA ' 94 (final score 6 - 1)

b.   Spanish Emilio Butragueno against Denmark in Mexico '86 (final score 5 - 1)

c.   Argentinian Mario Kempes against Peru in Argentina '78 (final score 6 - 0)

d.   Hungarian Ferenc Puskas against South Korea in Switzerland '54 (final score 9 - 0)

50.   **Who was the first person in world cup history to participate in the same tournament, both as coach and as player?**

a.   Franz Beckenbauer for West Germany (Mexico 1970).

b.   Willie Orman (Scotland 1954).

c.   Henry Michel for France (Mexico 1986).

d.   Mario Zagalo for Brazil (Chile 1962).

51. **Which of these players has scored more World Cup goals (not necessarily in the same tournament)?**

a. Justes Fontaine for France
b. Santor Kocsis for Hungary
c. Pele for Brazil
d. Gert Muller for W. Germany

52. **Which of these players was the 'heaviest' ever to champion - to receive a winner's medal?**

a. Jose Leao Andrade playing for Uruguay (1930)
b. Gordon Banks playing for England (1966)
c. Juergen Kohler playing for W.Germany (1990)
d. Rai playing for Brazil (1994)

53. **Which of these World Cup winning squads did NOT have any players from its domestic champion club, of that tournament's season?**

a. Uruguay (1930)
b. Italy (1934)
c. France (1998)
d. W.Germany (1974)

54. **Which are the only two national teams that have won a World Cup quarter-final match coming back from 3-0 down?**

a. W. Germany and Brazil
b. Portugal and Austria
c. Uruguay and Yugoslavia
d. U.S.S.R. and Mexico

55. **Which of these players was the youngest ever to participate in a World Cup finals tournament?**

a. Pele playing for Brazil (1958)
b. Tostao playing for Brazil (1966)
c. Eto ' o playing for Cameroon (1998)
d. Norman Whiteside playing for N.Ireland (1982)

56. **How has Diego Armando Maradona's first goal against England in the 1986 tournament been characterized?**

a. 'Hand of God'
b. 'Lucky Strike'
c. 'Hand of Diego'
d. 'Unfair Diego'

57. **Which of these players was the oldest champion - the oldest player to receive a World Cup winners medal?**

a. Bobby Charlton playing for England (1966)

b.   Klaus Augenthaler playing for W.Germany (1990)

c.   Nilton Santos playing for Brazil (1962)

d.   Dino Zoff playing for Italy (1982)

58.   In which of these World Cup finals did both finalists suffer a defeat earlier in the finals tournament?

a.   Italy v W. Germany 3-1 (1982)

b.   W. Germany v Netherlands 2-1 (1974)

c.   Brazil v Italy 0-0 (1994)

d.   Argentina v Netherlands 3-1 (1978)

59.   Which is the largest goal difference (goals for less goals against, all matches played) ever during a World Cup finals tournament?

a.   + 11

b.   + 14

c.   + 12

d.   + 17

60.   Who was the first Argentinian player to participate in 4 consecutive World Cup tournaments?

a.   Nestor Sensini

b.   Daniel Passarella

c.   Diego Armando Maradona

d.   Ubaldo Fillol

Answers Round 3

1. Hungary
2. Brazil
3. Franz Beckenbauer
4. Zinedine Zidane
5. West Germany
6. Penalties
7. Netherlands
8. 300
9. Bryan Robson
10. 1970
11. There were no qualification games
12. 3rd
13. Italy
14. True
15. Wankdorf Stadium
16. Hungary 8 Germany 3
17. Sweden
18. Jules Rimet Cup
19. Tofik Bachramov
20. Italy v Germany
21. Johan Neeskens
22. Holland lost in the final in both tournaments
23. Harald Schumacher
24. The Hand of God
25. Andreas Brehme
26. Roberto Baggio
27. Laurent Blanc
28. 2
29. Just Fontaine
30. Pele
31. Brazil
32. Seoul
33. Gerd Muller
34. Holland
35. Italy
36. Gigi Riva
37. India , Scotland and Turkey
38. Geoff Hurst for England (against West Germany in 1966).
39. Andreas Brehme
40. Uruguay v Argentina 4 - 2 (1930 Tournament)
41. 3-8
42. 2
43. Jules Rimet
44. Dirk Nanninga
45. Amarildo
46. Neeskens and Cruijff
47. Vittorio Pozzo
48. 3
49. Russian Oleg Salenko against Cameroon in USA ' 94 (final score 6 - 1)
50. Willie Orman (Scotland 1954).

51. Gert Muller for W. Germany

52. Rai playing for Brazil (1994)

53. France (1998)

54. Portugal and Austria

55. Norman Whiteside playing for N.Ireland (1982)

56. 'Hand of God'

57. Dino Zoff playing for Italy (1982)

58. Argentina v Netherlands 3-1 (1978)

59. + 17

60. Diego Armando Maradona

Round 4: UK Football Trivia

1. **England didn't enter the first three World Cups, but succeeded in qualifying for Brazil 1950, the first World Cup after World War II. Who was in their group?**
a. Mexico, Switzerland, and Argentina
b. Bolivia, Scotland, and Uruguay
c. Italy, Paraguay, and Sweden
d. Chile, Spain, and USA

2. **In which World Cup apart from 1966, did England progress furthest?**
a. Italy 1990
b. Japan & South Korea 2002
c. Mexico 1970
d. Mexico 1986

3. **In which of the following World Cups were England NOT eliminated by a penalty shootout?**
a. Italy 1990
b. Mexico 1970
c. France 1998
d. Germany 2006

4. **Who was the first England player to have won the Golden Boot, for the most goals scored in the tournament?**
a. Geoff Hurst
b. Bobby Charlton
c. David Platt
d. Gary Lineker

5. The 1958 World Cup in Sweden was the first World Cup in which all four home nations in the United Kingdom qualified, England, Scotland, Wales, and Northern Ireland. Out of these four, England progressed furthest.

a. True

b. False

6. Of course, the 1966 World Cup was the one that England fans look back on most proudly, the tournament that England both hosted, and won. Which of the following teams did England NOT play against on the road to winning the Cup?

a. France

b. Hungary

c. Mexico

d. Portugal

7. England player Geoff Hurst scored a hat-trick in the 1966 final against West Germany, and was the first player ever to do so in a World Cup final.

a. True

b. False

8. England were the defending champions in Mexico 1970, and in their second group match, they faced the 1958 and 1962 winners, Brazil. Ten minutes into the match, one of the Brazilians headed the ball at the goal, and goalkeeper Gordon Banks was forced to throw himself backwards and to the side to reach it, but he succeeded in deflecting the ball with his hand in what was widely regarded as one of the greatest saves ever. Which Brazilian player made that particular attempt on goal?

a. Carlos Alberto

b. Pele

c. Jairzinho

d. Gerson

9. In France 1998, one of the substitutes in the England squad was an 18-year old who was the youngest player to represent England in the 20th century. In England's second group game against Romania, he was brought off the bench and scored a goal seven minutes later. He was included in the starting lineup for England's top 16 match against Argentina, and in the 16th minute, he ran with the ball from the halfway line, dodged two Argentinians and scored a highly praised goal. Who was this young player?

a. Wayne Rooney

b. Michael Owen

c.   Theo Walcott
d.   Paul Scholes

10.   In the 2002 World Cup held in Japan and South Korea, England got revenge on Argentina for beating them in the 1986 and 1998 tournaments. They met in the group stage, and England won 1-0, but how was that single goal scored?

a.   A close-range header by Michael Owen
b.   An own goal by Gabriel Batistuta
c.   A volley by Paul Scholes
d.   A penalty by David Beckham

11.   Who has won most caps for England?

a.   Peter Shilton
b.   Bobby Moore
c.   Bobby Charlton
d.   Billy Wright

12.   Who was the first million pound transfer?

a.   Ian Rush
b.   Bryan Robson
c.   Trevor Francis
d.   Kevin Keegan

13.   Up to the end of the 1999-2000 how many clubs have won the FA Premier League?

a.   3
b.   5
c.   4
d.   6

14.   What was the first English club to win the European Cup?

a.   Aston Villa
b.   Liverpool
c.   Manchester United
d.   Arsenal

15.   True or False. Bobby Charlton has scored the most goals for England?

a.   True
b.   False

16.   Which English player scored the quickest goal in the final stages of the World Cup?

a.   Gary Lineker
b.   Bryan Robson

c. Bobby Charlton

d. Geoff Hurst

17.   Which two English clubs did George Best play for?

a. Manchester Utd and Tottenham

b. Manchester Utd and Fulham

c. Manchester City and Bolton

d. Manchester City and Fulham

18.   Who scored three goals for England in the World Cup final 1966?

a. Bobby Charlton

b. Geoff Hurst

c. Roger Hunt

d. Jimmy Grieves

19.   Which player was involved in a record breaking 15 million pound transfer between two English Clubs?

a. Alan Shearer

b. Chris Sutton

c. Dwight Yorke

d. Andy Cole

20.   Which premier league team play at St James Park?

a. Newcastle United

b. Middlesbrough

c. Sunderland

d. Coventry City

21.   Who captained England to World Cup glory in 1966?

a. Nobby Stiles

b. Bobby Charlton

c. Bobby Moore

d. Jack Charlton

22.   What were West Ham United formerly known as?

a. Upton Town F.C

b. Thames Ironworks F.C.

c. East London Steelworkers

d. Boleyn United

23.   Who was the first player to be sent off in a FA Cup Final?

a. Vinny Jones

b. Arthur Albiston

c. Mark Hughes

d. Kevin Moran

24.   How many England Managers were there in the 1990s?

a. 2

b. 3

c. 6

d. 7

25. **Which famous ex-professional Footballer became a top racehorse trainer?**

a. Tommy Smith

b. John-Jo O'Neil

c. Mick Channon

d. Tommy Docherty

26. **Who was the first ex-Celtic player (Catholic) to play for Glasgow Rangers as well?**

a. Frank McAvennie

b. Duncan Ferguson

c. Davie Cooper

d. Mo Johnston

27. **Where do Gillingham play their home games?**

a. Brisbane Road

b. Priestfield Stadium

c. Culverden Park

d. Mountfield Road

28. **Which of these players never captained England?**

a. Duncan Edwards

b. Billy Wright

c. Peter Shilton

d. David Beckham

29. **What was Kevin Keegan's nickname whilst he was playing in Germany?**

a. Afro

b. Mighty Mouse

c. Special K

d. Thumper

30. **Who were the last team from outside the Top Division to win the FA Cup?**

a. Brighton and Hove Albion

b. West Ham United

c. Manchester City

d. Queens Park Rangers

31. **Which of these teams was a founder team of the English Football League?**

a. Rotherham United
b. Manchester United
c. Everton
d. West Ham United

32. **Which English team supposedly gave Juventus, of Italy, the idea for their home strip?**

a. Grimsby Town
b. Darlington
c. Notts County
d. Newcastle United

33. **Who was the longest serving manager in English football in the 2003 season?**

a. Jim Smith
b. Sir Alex Ferguson
c. Dario Gradi
d. Trevor Francis

34. **What is the name of Birmingham City's ground?**

a. St. Michaels
b. St. Pauls
c. St. Peters
d. St. Andrews

35. **In which city would you find the Memorial Ground?**

a. Cardiff
b. Bristol
c. Birmingham
d. London

36. **Which footballer is nicknamed 'Sparky'?**

a. Ryan Giggs
b. Mark Hughes
c. Lee Hughes
d. Marian Pahars

37. **At which club did both John Gregory and Martin O'Neill start their managerial careers at?**

a. Rochdale
b. Wolverhampton Wanderers
c. Swindon Town
d. Wycombe Wanderers

38.   How many times did Gary Lineker get cautioned in his career?
a. 20
b. 16
c. 5
d. 0

39.   Who sponsors Sheffield Wednesday's kit?
a. They haven't got a kit sponsor
b. Hewlett Packard
c. Chupa Chups
d. Sanderson

40.   Who did Manchester United sign Bryan Robson from?
a. Chester
b. West Bromwich Albion
c. Cambridge United
d. No-one, he came through the Youth Academy

41.   For which English team did French goalkeeper Bernard Lama play for one season, in 1997-98?
a. Chelsea
b. West Ham United
c. Newcastle United
d. Arsenal

42.   For which team did Ronald De Boer play from 2000 to 2004?
a. Barcelona
b. AC Milan
c. Ajax
d. Glasgow Rangers

43.   Which Portugese team did Graeme Souness manage from 1997 to 1999?
a. Porto
b. Sporting Lisbon
c. Sporta Braga
d. Benfica

44.   Which of these players hasn't missed a penalty for England in a competitive tournament?
a. Gareth Southgate
b. Chris Waddle
c. Gary Lineker
d. Stuart Pearce

45.   Where did Millwall sign their goalkeeper Tony Warner from in 1999?

a. Wolverhampton Wanderers

b. Hull City

c. Arsenal

d. Liverpool

46. **Who signed for Aston Villa in 1998 and then, without playing a match, joined Everton?**

a. Richard Gough

b. David Unsworth

c. Danny Cadamateri

d. Paul Gerard

47. **Which English team did Louis Saha play for in the season 1999-2000?**

a. Arsenal

b. Fulham

c. West Ham United

d. Newcastle United

48. **Who was the first person in the history of the FA Premier League to have won both Carling awards: 'Manager of the Month' and 'Player of the Month'?**

a. Stuart Pearce

b. Graham Taylor

c. Alex Ferguson

d. George Graham

49. **What was Massimo Taibi's reason for getting 'megged' by Matt Le Tissier when playing goal-keeper for Manchester United in 1999-2000?**

a. His boots were too small

b. He was thinking about his wife who was in hospital

c. He got his studs caught in the turf

d. It was his birthday

50. **Who did theItalian Under-21 midfielder Enzo Maresca play for when in England before he moved to Juventus in 2000?**

a. Chelsea

b. West Bromwich Albion

c. Fulham

d. Nottingham Forest

Answers Round 4

1. Chile, Spain, and USA
2. Italy 1990
3. Mexico 1970
4. Gary Lineker
5. False
6. Hungary
7. True
8. Pele
9. Michael Owen
10. A penalty by David Beckham
11. Peter Shilton
12. Trevor Francis
13. 3
14. Manchester United
15. False
16. Bryan Robson
17. Manchester Utd and Fulham
18. Geoff Hurst
19. Alan Shearer
20. Newcastle United
21. Bobby Moore
22. Thames Ironworks F.C.
23. Kevin Moran
24. 6
25. Mick Channon
26. Mo Johnston
27. Priestfield Stadium
28. Duncan Edwards
29. Mighty Mouse
30. West Ham United
31. Everton
32. Notts County
33. Dario Gradi
34. St. Andrews
35. Bristol
36. Mark Hughes
37. Wycombe Wanderers
38. 0
39. Chupa Chups
40. West Bromwich Albion
41. West Ham United
42. Glasgow Rangers
43. Benfica
44. Gary Lineker
45. Liverpool
46. David Unsworth
47. Newcastle United
48. Stuart Pearce
49. He got his studs caught in the turf
50. West Bromwich Albion

Round 5: South American Football Trivia

1. Which two nations have won the tournament more times in the century?

a.   Argentina and Uruguay

b.   Chile and Brazil

c.   Brazil and Argentina

d.   Brazil and Uruguay

2. When was the first Copa America held?

a.   1915

b.   1920

c.   1916

d.   1922

3. Which one of this teams won the Copa America in the century?

a.   Chile

b.   Venezuela

c.   Ecuador

d.   Bolivia

4. Which was the first non-South American nation to the final?

a.   Japan

b.   USA

c.   Mexico

d.   Spain

5. Where was the 2004 cup held?

a.   Colombia

b.   Peru

c.   Venezuela

d.   Ecuador

6. When did Colombia win its first Copa America?

a.   1989

b.   1995

c.   2001

d.   1975

7. Which Brazilian player was 2004 goalie?

a.   Kaka

b.   Adriano

c.   Ronaldo

d.   Ronaldinho

8. Which of these was the biggest goal difference in a final?

a.   Argentina 8-0 Chile

b. Brazil 7-0 Paraguay

c. Uruguay 6-1 Paraguay

d. Brazil 5-0 Argentina

9. Which was the result of the final of 1995 cup?

a. Brazil 2-1 Uruguay

b. Uruguay 3-1 Brazil

c. Brazil 0-0 Uruguay (4-2 penalty shootout)

d. Uruguay 1-1 Brazil (5-3 penalty shootout)

10.   Uruguay had never lost a cup held in its territory in the 20th century.

a. True

b. False

11.   Which of the following broke the world record transfer fee in 1997?

a. Ronaldo

b. Denilson

c. Djalminha

d. Rivaldo

12.   Which of the following broke the world record transfer fee in 1998?

a. Denilson

b. Rivaldo

c. Djalminha

d. Ronaldo

13.   What is Ronaldo's full name?

a. Ronaldo Luiz Nazario da Lima

b. Ronaldo Rui Andre dos Santos

c. Ronaldo McDonaldo

d. Ronaldo Beto Cesario de Canoja

14.   Which of the following was the only one who was a member of the 2002 World Cup squad?

a. Romario

b. Evanilson

c. Elber

d. Ricardinho

15.   Which of the following scored in the 2002 Champions League Final?

a. Lucio

b. Roberto Carlos

c. Ze Roberto

d. Elber

16.   In the qualification for the 2002 World Cup, how many games did Brazil lose?

a. 0
b. 4
c. 6
d. 2

17.   What was the nickname of the 2002 World Cup coach, Luiz Felipe Scolari?

a. Big Phil
b. Lanky Loo
c. Puppet Master
d. Cinderella

18.   Which player dislocated his shoulder just prior to the start of the 2002 World Cup, and was sent home?

a. Emerson
b. Savio
c. Jardel
d. Fabio Rochemback

19.   Which of these players was described as 'The new Roberto Carlos'?

a. Ze Maria
b. Vampeta
c. Evanilson
d. Athirson

20.   Which Brazillian went on loan to Fiorentina from Inter Milan and scored six times in fifteen appearances during the 2001-02 season?

a. Adriano
b. Ewerthon
c. Luizao
d. Guilherme

21.   When did the argentinian Football change from amateur to professional Football?

a. 1930
b. 1931
c. 1928
d. 1934

22.   Who was the first champion of the pro Football?

a. Boca Juniors
b. Independiente
c. River Plate

d.   Racing Club

23.   Which team is known as the "King of Cups"?

a.   Independiente

b.   Boca Juniors

c.   River Plate

d.   Racing Club

24.   In which year, Gimnasia LP played the Libertadores Cup for the first time?

a.   2003

b.   1990

c.   2001

d.   1996

25.   Which of these stadiums had the bigger seating capacity in 2004?

a.   Racing Club

b.   Banfield

c.   Velez Sarsfield

d.   Rosario Central

26.   San Lorenzo won it's first Internacional Cup in 2001.

a.   True

b.   False

27.   How many goals did Arsenio Erico score?

a.   290

b.   293

c.   300

d.   250

28.   In which team did Crespo, Saviola, Aimar, Ortega, Almeida (they played more than 10 matches in Argentina National Team) make their debut in the Argentina Premier League?

a.   Boca Juniors

b.   San Lorenzo de Almagro

c.   Racing Club

d.   River Plate

29.   Supercopa. There were 9 editions of this Cup, the last in 1997. How many were won by Argentine Teams?

a.   2

b.   9

c.   6

d.   5

30.   When did the Argentina National Team win it's first World Cup?

a. 1986
b. 1978
c. 1982
d. 1974

Answers Round 5

1. Argentina and Uruguay
2. 1916
3. Bolivia
4. Mexico
5. Peru
6. 2001
7. Adriano
8. Brazil 7-0 Paraguay
9. Uruguay 1-1 Brazil (5-3 penalty shootout)
10. True
11. Ronaldo
12. Denilson
13. Ronaldo Luiz Nazario da Lima
14. Ricardinho
15. Lucio
16. 6
17. Big Phil
18. Emerson
19. Athirson
20. Adriano
21. 1931
22. Boca Juniors
23. Independiente
24. 2003
25. Racing Club
26. True
27. 293
28. River Plate
29. 6
30. 1978

Round 6: USA Soccer Trivia

1. **Which NASL team won the most championships?**
a.   Tampa Bay Rowdies
b.   Chicago Sting
c.   Tulsa Roughnecks
d.   New York Cosmos

2. **One more Cosmos question. List a stadium the Comsos DID NOT use as their home field during their NASL history?**
a.   Giants Stadium
b.   Shea Stadium
c.   Downing Stadium
d.   Hofstra U. Stadium

3. **Which NASL franchise lasted the longest without changing its city or nickname?**
a.   Dallas Tornado
b.   Ft. Lauderdale Strikers
c.   New York Cosmos
d.   Toronto Blizzard

4. **As of the 2001 season, which of the following is the only Major League Soccer city or market to never host a NASL team?**
a.   Kansas City, MO
b.   Denver, Colorado
c.   Columbus, Ohio
d.   Miami, Florida

5. **As of the 2001 season, what is the only MLS team to have the exact name of it's NASL namesake?**
a.   Chicago Fire
b.   NY-NJ Metrostars
c.   San Jose Earthquakes
d.   Los Angeles Galaxy

6. **What is the NASL's longest surviving franchise, in spite of name changes and relocations (final names listed as choices)?**
a.   Toronto Blizzard
b.   Minnesota Strikers
c.   New York Cosmos
d.   California Surf

7. **Where did Team America call home in it's only season in 1983?**

a. New York

b. Washington

c. St. Louis

d. Houston

8. To what city did the Phildelphia Fury relocate in 1981?

a. Montreal

b. Kansas City

c. Oakland

d. Vancouver

9. Which of the following was a city or market that was NEVER home to an NASL franchise?

a. Honolulu

b. Phoenix

c. San Antonio

d. Jacksonville

10.   How many NASL teams competed in its last season in 1984?

a. 7

b. 9

c. 12

d. 10

11.   At one point, from 1978-1979, the NASL had as many as _____ teams!

a. 28

b. 24

c. 32

d. 20

12.   The Kansas City Wizards are the 2000 NASL champions. What was the name of the other team from Kansas City that won the NASL crown in 1969?

a. Cowboys

b. Royals

c. Spurs

d. Kings

13.   This NASL franchise left this city, then came back!

a. Baltimore Bays

b. St. Louis Stars

c. San Diego Jaws

d. Ft. Lauderale Strikers

14.   Where did the New England Tea Men relocate?

a. New Jersey

b. Jacksonville

c. Edmonton

d. Calgary

15.   This team went on to win the most Major Indoor Soccer League championships in that league's history:

a. Baltimore Blast

b. San Diego Sockers

c. Minnesota Strikers

d. Chicago Sting

16.   What two teams duked it out for the NASL title on October 3, 1984 in the last NASL game ever?

a. San Diego Sockers vs. Baltimore Blast

b. Cosmos vs. Vancouver Whitecaps

c. Chicago Sting v. Toronto Blizzard

d. Tampa Bay Rowdies vs. Tulsa Roughnecks

17.   Which team holds the NASL record for most wins in an NASL regular season?

a. New York Cosmos

b. Seattle Sounders

c. Vancouver Whitecaps

d. Detroit Express

18.   What is the only other NASL team besides the Cosmos to report an average season attendance of over 30,000?

a. Seattle Sounders

b. Tampa Bay Rowdies

c. Vancouver Whitecaps

d. Minnesota Kicks

19.   How many New York Cosmos players won the NASL MVP?

a. 5

b. 1

c. 0

d. 12

20.   Which team set an NASL record in 1981 for losses in a single season, with 27?

a. Dallas Tornado

b. Colorado Caribou

c. Philadelphia Fury

d. Detroit Express

21.   Korea 2002: USA vs Portugal: In the 4th minute, Brian McBride's header was blocked by Vitor Baia. Who collected the rebound and scored?

a.   Joe-Max Moore
b.   Demarcus Beasley
c.   Landon Donovan
d.   John O' Brien

22.   Korea 2002: USA vs Portugal: After an atrocious Portuguese giveaway, Landon Donovan's shot deflected off the head of a Portuguese defender, and into the back of the net. Who scored the Own Goal in the 30th Minute?

a.   Rui Jorge
b.   Fernando Couto
c.   Jorge Costa
d.   Beto

23.   Korea 2002: USA vs Portugal: In the 36th minute, who headed in Tony Sanneh's cross?

a.   Earnie Stewart
b.   Brian McBride
c.   Landon Donovan
d.   John O' Brien

24.   Korea 2002: USA vs South Korea: In the 24th minute, who scored from a perfect ball from John O' Brien?

a.   Clint Mathis
b.   Brian McBride
c.   Demarcus Beasley
d.   Claudio Reyna

25.   Korea 2002: USA vs South Korea: In the 39th Minute, Jeff Agoos brought down Hwang-Sun Hong in the box, and South Korea were awarded a penalty. Who took the kick, which was saved by Brad Friedel?

a.   Ahn Jung Hwan
b.   Lee Eul Yong
c.   Seol Ki Hyeon
d.   Park Ji Sung

26.   Korea 2002: USA vs South Korea: South Korea got the equaliser in the 78th minute. Who scored off of Lee Eul Yong's free kick?

a.   Ahn Jung Hwan
b.   Hong Myung Bo
c.   Lee Chun Soo
d.   Choi Yong Soo

27.   **Korea 2002: USA vs Poland: The match got off to a nightmare start. In the 3rd minute, who scored off the clearance of his own header?**
a. Cezary Kucharski
b. Jacek Krzynowek
c. Emmanuel Olisadebe
d. Maciej Zurawski

28.   **Korea 2002: USA vs Poland: The nightmare continued. Landon Donovan's goal was disallowed for pushing, and then Poland took a 2-0 lead. Who converted Jacek Krzynowek's cross?**
a. Emmanuel Olisadebe
b. Pawel Kryszalowicz
c. Marcin Zewlakow
d. Maciej Zurawski

29.   **Korea 2002: USA vs Poland: An hour later, the USA found themselves down 3-0, and all eyes turned to Incheon where South Korea were playing Portugal. Needing only a draw to win the group, South Korea beat a 9-man Portugal side on a 70th minute goal. Who scored the goal that put the Americans through to the round of 16?**
a. Yoo Sang Chul
b. Ahn Jung Hwan
c. Park Ji Sung
d. Seol Ki Hyeon

30.   **Korea 2002: 10As runners up in Group D, the USA's round of 16 opponents would be the Group G winners Mexico. The game got off to a great start for the Americans. In the 8th minute, who scored his second goal of the tournament?**
a. Landon Donovan
b. Clint Mathis
c. John O' Brien
d. Brian McBride

31.   **Korea 2002: USA vs Mexico (round of 15): In the 65th minute, the USA went 2-0 up. Who headed in Eddie Lewis' cross?**
a. Brian McBride
b. Landon Donovan
c. Demarcus Beasley
d. Clint Mathis

32.   Korea 2002: USA vs Mexico, With the USA nursing a 2-0 lead, manager Bruce Arena brought in veteran Cobi Jones for Brian McBride in the 79th minute. Less than 10 minutes later, Cobi was headbutted and Mexico were a man down. Which Mexican player was sent off in the 88th minute?

a.   Rafael Márquez
b.   Alberto García Aspe
c.   Salvador Carmona
d.   Cuauthémoc Blanco

33.   Korea 2002: USA vs Germany: The match got off to an encouraging start, as the USA had plenty of early chances. In the 39th minute, Eddie Lewis fouled Torsten Frings on the right-flank. Who scored for Germany on Christian Ziege's free kick?

a.   Bernd Schneider
b.   Miroslav Klose
c.   Michael Ballack
d.   Oliver Neuville

34.   USA vs Germany: The most controversial moment of the USA's World Cup came in the 51st minute. Gregg Berhalter volleyed a Cobi Jones corner kick, it beat Oliver Kahn, and the ball hit a German player on the hand, failing to cross the goal line. The Americans wanted a spot kick, but referee Hugh Dallas turned down their appeals. Which German player was accused of handling the ball in the box?

a.   Christian Ziege
b.   Torsten Frings
c.   Thomas Linke
d.   Sebastian Kehl

35.   The match ended Germany 1 - 0 USA, and the Americans' world cup dream was over. Which USA player was selected to the 2002 FIFA World Cup All-Star team?

a.   Landon Donovan
b.   Brad Friedel
c.   Claudio Reyna
d.   Brian McBride

36.   Which teams played in the first Soccer Bowl?

a.   New York Cosmos and Seattle Sounders
b.   Tampa Bay Rowdies and Portland Timbers
c.   Minnesota Kicks and Dallas Tornado

d.   Washington Diplomats and Los Angeles Aztecs

37.   **In Soccer Bowl 76, held in Seattle's Kingdome, the Minnesota Kicks took on Toronto's NASL entry. What was the team's nickname?**

a.   Toronto Blizzard

b.   Toronto Metros-Croatia

c.   Toronto Shooting Stars

d.   Toronto Soccer Maple Leafs

38.   **In Soccer Bowl 77, Pele's last competitive match, who scored the Cosmos goals in their 2-1 victory over the Seattle Sounders?**

a.   Pele and Bobby Smith

b.   Dennis Teuart and Franz Beckenbauer

c.   Steve Hunt and Giorgio Chinaglia

d.   Rick Davis and Vladislav Bogicevic

39.   **In Soccer Bowl 78 the Cosmos came home to Giants Stadium for the final. A rousing 3-1 victory led by Dennis Teuart. Who were the opponents?**

a.   Portland Timbers

b.   Ft. Lauderdale Strikers

c.   San Diego Sockers

d.   Tampa Bay Rowdies

40.   **Soccer Bowl 79 saw the Rowdies return to Giants Stadium to take on Vancouver Whitecaps, only to drop another championship, 2-1. Who did the Whitecaps defeat to get to the finals?**

a.   New York Cosmos

b.   Tulsa Roughnecks

c.   Oakland Stompers

d.   Houston Hurricane

41.   **From 1975-1982 the Soccer Bowl got the attention of national tv. ABC and TSN, a sports syndicator, televised five of the matches. Who televised the other three?**

a.   ESPN and NBC

b.   CBS and USA

c.   NBC and PBS

d.   PBS and CBS

42.   **Where was Soccer Bowl '80 played?**

a.   Toronto's Exhibition Stadium

b.   Vancouver's BC Place

c.   Washington's RFK Stadium

d.   Portland's Civic Stadium

43.   In Soccer Bowl '81 what happened that had ever happened before in Soccer Bowl history up to that point?
a.   The game was decided on a shootout.
b.   The game was decided in overtime.
c.   There was a shutout.
d.   The game was rained out and decided by a coin toss.

44.   In the Soccer Bowl of 1983 Toronto Blizzard faced off with the Tulsa entry, what was their nickname?
a.   Roughnecks
b.   Cowboys
c.   Oilers
d.   Sooners

45.   In the 1984 Soccer Bowl Chicago Sting played Toronto Blizzard for the league title. What made this another first for the NASL?
a.   It was the first Soccer Bowl televised in prime time
b.   The Soccer Bowl was a series instead of one game
c.   It was the first Soccer Bowl to have a total of 10 goals
d.   It was the first time two brothers were opposing coaches

46.   Which Seattle Sounders forward scored a hat trick in England's 1966 World Cup Final victory?
a.   Geoff Hurst
b.   Johan Cruyuff
c.   George Best
d.   Andy Cole

47.   In one of the most amazing performances in NASL history, and maybe soccer history, he scored 18 goals in 7 playoff games, including 7 in one game vs. the Tulsa Roughnecks. Who is he?
a.   Pele
b.   Tatu
c.   Franz Beckenbauer
d.   Giorgio Chinaglia

48.   Who is the only player to win the NASL MVP award twice?
a.   Pele
b.   Johan Cruyuff
c.   Giorgio Chinaglia
d.   Carlos Metidieri

49.   Who scored more goals than anyone else in NASL history?
a.   Giorgia Chinaglia
b.   Karl Heinz-Granitza

c.   Alan Wiley

d.   Pele

50.   How many total goals did Pele score in the NASL, including playoffs?

a.   39

b.   80

c.   117

d.   150

51.   Who scored more assists than any other NASL player?

a.   Vladislav Bogicevic

b.   Giorgio Chinaglia

c.   Pele

d.   Kyle Rote, Jr.

52.   Who holds the record for most goals scored in an NASL regular season?

a.   Karl Heinz Granitza

b.   Pele

c.   Giorgio Chinaglia

d.   Alan Wiley

53.   What goalie holds the NASL record for most shutouts in one regular seaon?

a.   Jack Brand

b.   Tino Lattieri

c.   Bob Rigby

d.   Tony Shumacher

54.   Which of the following statements is true about Pele's last game, played in October 1977?

a.   All of these are correct

b.   Pele played for both teams

c.   Pele scored

d.   Held at Giants Stadium

55.   Despite being the third highest goal scorer in NASL history, he was never named to an NASL All-Star team. Who is he?

a.   Franz Beckenbauer

b.   Kyle Rote, Jr.

c.   Pele

d.   Karl Heinz-Granitza

56.   The 2008 Chicago Fire played in what stadium in Bridgeview, Illinois?

a.   Soldier Field

b.   Toyota Park

c.   Wrigley Field

d.   US Cellular Field

57.   San Jose Earthquakes were an inaugural team back in 1996, however they were relocated to Houston in 2005. Forunately, the Earthquakes' name was brought back to San Jose in 2008. Which of the following is a stadium in which they did not play?

a.   Spartan Stadium

b.   McAfee Stadium

c.   Monster Park

d.   Buck Shaw Stadium

58.   DC United uses Robert F. Kennedy Stadium for their home games. In 2008, with whom did DC United share their stadium?

a.   Washington Wizards

b.   Washington Nationals

c.   No one

d.   Washington Redskins

59.   In 2008, Rice-Eccles Stadium housed which MLS team for their home games?

a.   Colorado Rapids

b.   Houston Dynamo

c.   Real Salt Lake

d.   Toronto FC

60.   Which team, known as America's hardest working team, had the first soccer-specific stadium in the United States?

a.   Columbus Crew

b.   FC Dallas

c.   DC United

d.   Houston Dynamo

61.   FC Dallas, founded as the Dallas Burn in 1996, played their home games in what stadium in 2008?

a.   The Home Depot Center

b.   Dick's Sporting Goods Park

c.   BMO Field

d.   Pizza Hut Park

62.   Which MLS team shared their home stadium with their city's T-Bones baseball team in 2008?

a.   Kansas City Wizards

b.   LA Galaxy

c. Colorado Rapids

d. San José Earthquakes

63. **The Houston Dynamo uses Robertson Stadium, a football stadium on the campus of what university?**

a. San Jacinto College

b. Rice University

c. University of Houston

d. University of Texas

64. **Who played in the Home Depot Center?**

a. Chivas USA

b. Both of Them

c. LA Galaxy

d. Neither of Them

65. **In 2008, New York Red Bulls played their home games in what stadium?**

a. Shea Stadium

b. Rutgers Stadium

c. Yankee Stadium

d. Giants Stadium

Answers Round 6

1. New York Cosmos
2. Shea Stadium
3. Dallas Tornado
4. Columbus, Ohio
5. San Jose Earthquakes
6. Minnesota Strikers
7. Washington
8. Montreal
9. Phoenix
10. 9
11. 24
12. Spurs
13. San Diego Jaws
14. Jacksonville
15. San Diego Sockers
16. Chicago Sting v. Toronto Blizzard
17. Seattle Sounders
18. Minnesota Kicks
19. 5
20. Dallas Tornado
21. John O' Brien
22. Jorge Costa
23. Brian McBride

24. Clint Mathis
25. Lee Eul Yong
26. Ahn Jung Hwan
27. Emmanuel Olisadebe
28. Pawel Kryszalowicz
29. Park Ji Sung
30. Brian McBride
31. Landon Donovan
32. Rafael Márquez
33. Michael Ballack
34. Torsten Frings
35. Claudio Reyna
36. Tampa Bay Rowdies and Portland Timbers
37. Toronto Metros-Croatia
38. Steve Hunt and Giorgio Chinaglia
39. Tampa Bay Rowdies
40. New York Cosmos
41. CBS and USA
42. Washington's RFK Stadium
43. The game was decided on a shootout.
44. Roughnecks
45. The Soccer Bowl was a series instead of one game
46. Geoff Hurst
47. Giorgio Chinaglia
48. Carlos Metidieri
49. Giorgia Chinaglia
50. 39
51. Vladislav Bogicevic
52. Giorgio Chinaglia
53. Jack Brand
54. All of these are correct
55. Karl Heinz-Granitza
56. Toyota Park
57. Monster Park
58. No one
59. Real Salt Lake
60. Columbus Crew
61. Pizza Hut Park
62. Kansas City Wizards
63. University of Houston
64. Both of Them
65. Giants Stadium

Round 7:World Football Challenge Trivia

1. In February 2005, Arsenal faced Manchester United at Highbury. It was a typically passionate affair with captains Roy Keane and Patrick Viera famously clashing in the tunnel before the game had even got underway. But which full-back grabbed a late goal to ensure his team were victorious with a delightful left-footed chip over the goalkeeper?
   a. Ashley Cole
   b. Gabriel Heinze
   c. Mikael Silvestre
   d. John O'Shea

2. In the final set of fixtures of the 2002 World Cup group stages, Brazil faced off against Costa Rica, with a place in the last 16 guaranteed to the winner. Unsurprisingly, the four times champions emerged triumphant on their way to a record fifth world cup. But the goal of the game, and perhaps the tournament, was scored by which defender in spectacular style?
   a. Lucio
   b. Cafu
   c. Junior
   d. Edmilson

3. One of the goals of the tournament at the 1994 World Cup was scored against Belgium in the group stages by a player from an unlikely country. This player took control of the ball in his own half, weaved around five Belgian players and sent the ball skying into the top corner of the net. But which nation did this unheard of player hail from?
   a. Saudi Arabia
   b. Bolivia
   c. Morocco
   d. Cameroon

4. This goal was the 1996-97 BBC Match of the Day "Goal of the Season", and was scored in the FA Cup 4th round against Barnsley by a winger. It was a spectacular overhead kick from just outside the edge of the box. Which player scored this acrobatic effort?
   a. Andrei Kanchelskis
   b. Marc Overmars

c.   Trevor Sinclair

d.   Anders Limpar

5. This screaming curler was scored by one of Brazil's right-backs in the 1970s. It was scored in the 3rd place play-off in the 1978 World Cup against Italy, but which of the following scored it?

a.   Edinho

b.   Carlos Alberto

c.   Nelinho

d.   Eder

6. This stunning strike was scored by an England international against Hungary in 1981 and was so cleanly hit that it got stuck in the stanchion of the goal. Which classy midfielder scored this effort?

a.   Trevor Brooking

b.   Steve Coppell

c.   Kevin Keegan

d.   Bryan Robson

7. This absolutely scorching goal was hit from 30+ yards on a muddy pitch in an FA Cup 3rd Round replay game against Newcastle United in 1972. The player who struck the goal caused one of the biggest FA cup upsets in history and led his team Hereford United into the 4th round. But what was his name?

a.   Charlie George

b.   Ronnie Radford

c.   Peter Lorimer

d.   Ray Crawford

8. Who was the Republic of Ireland's unlikely goalscoring hero in their 2nd round penalty shoot-out in the 1990 World Cup against Romania, scoring the winning penalty after the Romanians' previous penalty had been saved by Pat Bonner?

a.   David O'Leary

b.   Ray Houghton

c.   Tony Cascarino

d.   Steve Staunton

9. Who scored a brace on his England debut in 2005, including a cracking free-kick but did not manage to solidify his place in the team in the subsequent few years?

a.   Francis Jeffers

b.   Kieran Richardson

c.   Andy Johnson

d.   Jermaine Jenas

10.   **What is the name of the player who responded to an appeal via teletext for strikers, and ended up scoring a last-gasp winner in February 2001, in an FA cup quarter final to knock out Leicester City, after coming on as a late substitute?**

a.   Gary Bailey

b.   Jimmy Glass

c.   Roy Essandoh

d.   Brian Howard

11.   **Argentine keeper Carlos Roa retired from football in 1999 despite being at his peak. For what reason did he retire?**

a.   He had to have his arm amputated after a nasty car crash

b.   He was a Seventh Day Adventist and believed the World would end at the turn of the millenium

c.   His wife believed he was neglecting his kids whilst playing football

d.   He wanted to pursue his passion for opera professionally

12.   **Which goalie once injured his penis whilst playing a 5-a-side charity game against Iron Maiden?**

a.   Antonio Prats

b.   Bernard Lama

c.   Ronald Watteraus

d.   Mart Poom

13.   **Which goalie retired with a career goals total of 63?**

a.   Rene Higuita

b.   Rogerio Ceni

c.   Hans Jorg-Butt

d.   Jose Luis Chilavert

14.   **Which English keeper played his last game in 1997 for Leyton Orient, after a staggering 31-year career?**

a.   Peter Shilton

b.   Ray Clemence

c.   John Burridge

d.   Mervyn Day

15.   **Which goalie was arrested for an involvement in a kidnapping?**

a.   Rene Higuita

b.   German Burgos

c.   Oscar Cordoba

d.   Ricardo Tavarelli

16.   Who was the first keeper to save a penalty in an English FA Cup final?

a.   Erik Thorstvedt
b.   Steve Ogrizovic
c.   Dave Beasant
d.   Nigel Spink

17.   Which controversial spiritualist was once a professional goalkeeper?

a.   David Icke
b.   Johnathan Edwards
c.   Derek Acorah
d.   Shirley Ghostman

18.   What was the name of the Manchester United keeper whose career lasted just over a minute?

a.   Nick Culkin
b.   Ron Robert-Zieler
c.   Paul Rachubka
d.   Ben Foster

19.   Who was the heroic Argentine keeper who replaced the unfortunate Nery Pumpido in Italia 90?

a.   Hector Zalada
b.   Angel Comizzo
c.   Sergio Goycochea
d.   Luis Islas

20.   Which keeper used to design his own shirts?

a.   Fabian Barthez
b.   Jorge Campos
c.   Filip De Wilde
d.   Andy Goram

21.   The Liverpool home shirt is what colour?

a.   Pink
b.   Blue
c.   Red
d.   Red and Blue

22.   The Aston Villa home shirt is what colour?

a.   Green
b.   Claret and Blue
c.   Yellow and Black
d.   Red and Blue

23.   Queens Park Rangers have hooped home shirts, but what colour are these hoops?
a.   Black and White
b.   Yellow and Blue
c.   Red and Green
d.   Blue and White

24.   Which three teams have home shirts that are black and white?
a.   Juventus, Newcastle, and Walsall
b.   Newcastle United, Grimsby Town, and Gillingham Town
c.   Notts County, Swansea City, and Juventus
d.   Juventus, Reading, and Scunthorpe United

25.   The Darlington home shirt is what colour?
a.   White
b.   Black and White
c.   Red and Black
d.   Red

26.   Tottenham Hotspur's away shirt is what colour?
a.   White
b.   Royal Blue
c.   Pale Blue
d.   Yellow

27.   The Oxford United home shirt is what colour?
a.   White
b.   Red
c.   Yellow
d.   Blue

28.   When Manchester United won the European Cup in 1999, what colour shirts were they wearing?
a.   Black
b.   Red
c.   White
d.   Grey

29.   Sau Paulo F.C. have three colours on their home shirts, what are they?
a.   White, Black and Yellow
b.   White, Red and Grey
c.   Red, White and Black
d.   Red, White and Blue

30.   Which of these clubs does not have yellow on their home shirts?

a. ADO Den Haag

b. Galatasaray

c. Dynamo Kiev

d. Torquay United

31.   Which pop star's uncle scored the winning goal in the 1959 FA Cup final?

a. Sting

b. Elton John

c. Noddy Holder

d. Simon Le Bon

32.   Which was the smallest city to host a club that has won the European Cup in 2001?

a. Dortmund

b. Nottingham

c. Eindhoven

d. Turin

33.   Who supplied the cross which Pele headed down, only for Gordon Banks to make 'the greatest ever save'?

a. Carlos Alberto

b. Jairzinho

c. Tostao

d. Rivelino

34.   Which was the last Scottish team to win a major European trophy (as of the end of 2000-01 season)?

a. Aberdeen

b. Glasgow Rangers

c. Glasgow Celtic

d. Dundee United

35.   What position did Luciano Pavarotti (one of the 3 tenors) play in his younger days?

a. Striker

b. Goalkeeper

c. Midfielder

d. Bench warmer

36.   For which club did Rod Stewart have a trial with, as a an 18 year old youth?

a. Celtic

b. Leyton Orient

c. Stirling Albion

d.   Brentford

37.   **What colour kits did Juventus originally play in?**

a.   Maroon

b.   Black and White

c.   Pink

d.   Sky Blue

38.   **Who scored 'the other' of England's 4 goals in the 1966 World Cup final, against West Germany?**

a.   Roger Hunt

b.   Martin Peters

c.   Bobby Charlton

d.   Alan Ball

39.   **Who was the last team to win the Football League title before the First Division became the FA Premier League?**

a.   Arsenal

b.   Leeds United

c.   Liverpool

d.   Manchester United

40.   **Who captained Fulham to an FA Cup Final during the 1970s?**

a.   George Best

b.   Bobby Moore

c.   Rodney Marsh

d.   Gerry Francis

41.   **What have Herbert Chapman, Brian Clough and Kenny Dalglish got in common (as managers)?**

a.   They have all won each of the domestic trophies, except the FA cup.

b.   They have all won the league as player managers.

c.   Each of them has been made a freeman of a city.

d.   They have all won the English league title with 2 different clubs.

42.   **Who scored a hatrick in the memorable 1998 first division playoff final, where Charlton Athletic beat Sunderland on penalties after a thrilling 4-4 draw?**

a.   Jonathon Hunt

b.   Clive Mendonca

c.   Kevin Phillips

d.   'Big' Niall Quinn

43.   **Who scored Brazil's 100th goal in world cup finals matches?**

a.   Carlos Alberto

b.   Pele

c. Jairzinho

d. Rivelino

44.   Who scored 5 goals in a match, but still ended up on the losing team?

a. Dennis Law

b. Trevor Francis

c. Alan Clarke

d. Paul Mariner

45.   Which of these players has saved a penalty for Manchester City in a mid-1990s league match?

a. David White

b. Keith Curle

c. Gary Flitcroft

d. Niall Quinn

46.   As well as scoring prolifically for Red Bull Salzburg, striker Erling Braut Haaland scored 9 goals in Norway's 12-0 win v Honduras at the FIFA U-20 World Cup in May 2019. He also was the first teenager to score in five consecutive matches in the European Champions League, achieved during 2019-20 competition. Where was Erling born on 21 July 2000?

a. Oslo, Norway

b. Salzburg, Austria

c. Bryne, Norway

d. Leeds, England

47.   Counting only officially sanctioned games which of these four players scored the most goals during his career?

a. Puskas, Ferenc (Hungary)

b. Josef Bican, Austria

c. Romario (Brazil)

d. Pele (Brazil)

48.   The scorer of the first hat-trick in a World Cup Final was playing for a domestic club that supplied three players to the World Cup winning side that day. Can you name the club?

a. West Ham United

b. Santos

c. Stoke City

d. Barcelona

49.	Out of the four players, who was the youngest when scoring his first English Premier League goal?

a.	James Milner -Leeds United
b.	Cesc Fabregas - Arsenal
c.	Wayne Rooney - Everton
d.	James Vaughan - Everton

50.	Which of these former Scottish legends has scored the most international goals for Scotland?

a.	Hughie Gallacher
b.	Denis Law
c.	Julie Fleeting
d.	Kenny Dalglish

51.	Who was the first player to score hat-tricks in the Premier League, all three divisions of the English Football League, the League Cup, the FA Cup, and for his country in an international match?

a.	Didier Drogba
b.	Jason Roberts
c.	Teddy Sheringham
d.	Robert Earnshaw

52.	Which of these four players scored the quickest Premier League hat-trick?

a.	Thiery Henry
b.	Ole Gunnar Solskjær
c.	Sadio Mané
d.	Robbie Fowler

53.	Which player scored a goal in only 7.69 seconds at Vicarage Road during a English premiership league game in April 2019?

a.	Alan Shearer - for Newcastle United v Manchester City
b.	Ledley King - for Spurs against Bradford City
c.	Shane Long - for Southampton against Watford
d.	Christian Eriksen - for Spurs against Manchester Utd

54.	The European Golden Boot is an award that is presented each season to the leading goalscorer in league matches from the top division of all European national leagues. Who was the first player to win this trophy six times?

a.	Cristiano Ronaldo
b.	Thierry Henry
c.	Lionel Messi
d.	Luis Suárez

55.   Which club was the first to score 950 goals in European Champions Cup/European Champions League games?

a. Manchester United
b. Bayern Munich
c. Real Madrid
d. Barcelona

56.   In what year was Glenn Hoddle born?

a. 1958
b. 1957
c. 1959
d. 1960

57.   This man won the European Footballer of the Year award in back-to-back years in 1978 and 1979. Who was he?

a. Bobby Robson
b. David Moyes
c. Glen Hoddle
d. Kevin Keegan

58.   Which year was the first FA Cup live in colour on TV?

a. 1969
b. 1966
c. 1967
d. 1968

59.   Which 3 clubs had Sir Alex Ferguson managed before Manchester United?

a. Ayr, Queen's Park, Aberdeen
b. Stirling Albion, St. Mirren, Aberdeen
c. East Stirling, St. Miren, Aberdeen
d. Stenhousemeuir, Ross County, Aberdeen

60.   In the 1889 FA Cup Final, Preston North End beat which club to complete the first ever double?

a. Accrington Stanley
b. Wolverhampton Wanderers
c. Burnley
d. Newton Heath

61.   On 25th January, 1964, Doncaster Rovers beat Darlington 10-0, but in what division was this game played?

a. Old 3rd North
b. Old 2nd
c. Old 4th

d.   Old 3rd South

62.   **Which four teams competed in the play-offs of the 1995-96 season in Division 1?**

a.   Barnsley, Watford, Norwich City, Fulham
b.   Ipswich Town, Sheffield United, West Brom, Birmingham City
c.   Crystal Palace, Stoke City, Leicester City, Charlton Athletic
d.   Bolton Wanderers, Middlesbrough, QPR, Wolves

63.   **Who finished in third place in the last season of the old 1st Division?**

a.   QPR
b.   Aston Villa
c.   Leeds United
d.   Sheffield Wednesday

64.   **How many different teams had won the original first Division before it was transfered into the Premier League?**

a.   23
b.   33
c.   22
d.   32

65.   **When Manchester United won their record 9th FA Cup final in 1995-96, they beat Liverpool in the final, but who did Liverpool beat 7-0 in the 3rd round?**

a.   Rochdale United
b.   Oldham Athletic
c.   Burnley
d.   Oxford City

66.   **Peter Schmeichel played in goal for Manchester United in the FA Cup final of 1993?**

a.   True
b.   False

67.   **How many times was the FA Cup Final contested at Kennington Oval?**

a.   15
b.   19
c.   0
d.   20

68.   **Who won the Scottish Premier Division in 1978-79?**

a.   Dundee United
b.   Rangers
c.   Celtic

d.   Aberdeen

69.   Which 2 teams dominated the Scottish FA Cup between 1874 and 1882?

a.   Celtic, Rangers

b.   Queens Park, Vale of Leven

c.   Clydesdale, Renton

d.   Third Lanark, Thornlibank

70.   Who won the Welsh Cup in 1995-1996?

a.   Wrexham

b.   Swansea City

c.   Bangor City

d.   TNS LLansantffraid

71.   Who won the FA Woman's National Division in 1995-1996?

a.   Doncaster Belles

b.   Wembley

c.   Millwall Lionesses

d.   Croydon

72.   Who were the first English side to lose in an European Cup Final?

a.   Leeds United

b.   Aston Villa

c.   Liverpool

d.   Manchester United

73.   Who were Rangers' opponents in the first ever Cup Winner's Cup Final?

a.   AC Milan

b.   Roma

c.   Fiorentina

d.   Inter Milan

74.   Who were the champions of Malta in season 1995-1996?

a.   Sliema Wanderers

b.   Widzew Lodz

c.   Pyounic Yerevan

d.   HIT Gorica

75.   In which League group were England placed in the first stage of Euro 96?

a.   A

b.   C

c.   B

d.   D

76.   **What is the nickname of the Rangers player, Jorg Albertz?**
a.   The Rock
b.   The German Bomber
c.   The Hammer
d.   The Terminator

77.   **Which is the only club to appear in both League Cup Finals sponsored by Rumbelows?**
a.   Nottingham Forest
b.   Manchester United
c.   Arsenal
d.   Chelsea

78.   **What is the highest position Luton Town have ever achieved in the top division?**
a.   7th
b.   13th
c.   10th
d.   15th

79.   **The book Macca Can was about which player?**
a.   Malcolm MacDonald
b.   Steve McMahon
c.   Alan McInally
d.   Steve McManaman

80.   **Which French team are known as Les Verts (The Greens)?**
a.   Strasbourg
b.   Nantes
c.   Montpellier
d.   St Etienne

81.   **What is the christian name of the Spain and Real Madrid defender, Hierro?**
a.   Jose
b.   Fernando
c.   Sebastien
d.   Roberto

82.   **If you went to see IA Akranes play - which country would you go to?**
a.   Latvia
b.   Finland
c.   Belarus
d.   Iceland

83.   Which team did Mark McGhee win European honours with?

a.   Aberdeen

b.   Celtic

c.   Cologne

d.   Porto

84.   Which international side did Claudio Caniggia play for?

a.   Portugal

b.   Colombia

c.   Argentina

d.   Italy

85.   Which club did Paul Rideout leave to join Everton?

a.   Bari

b.   Rangers

c.   Aston Villa

d.   Swindon Town

86.   Who missed 3 penalties for Argentina in the 1999 Copa America match against Colombia?

a.   Claudio Lopez

b.   Gabriel Batistuta

c.   Martin Palermo

d.   Juan Veron

87.   Why was Willie Henderson absent from the Rangers line up for the 1962 tie against Standard Liege?

a.   He didn't play for Rangers at the time.

b.   Missed the kick off after heavy traffic held him up in Glasgow

c.   He was arrested on his way to the game.

d.   He fell down the stairs in his home before the game and injured himself.

88.   Who was voted the best player in the 2000 King Hussein Cup?

a.   Ali Karimi

b.   Ali Al-Jaber

c.   Ali Daei

d.   Ali Hussein

89.   Which goalkeeper replaced the injured Gianluigi Buffon in the Italy Squad for Euro 2000?

a.   Christian Abbiati

b.   Francesco Toldo

c.   Luca Bucci

d.   Angelo Peruzzi

90. **How many of Norway's Euro 2000 squad played their club football in Britain at the time of the tournament?**
a. 10
b. 9
c. 8
d. 7

91. **Which club play their home matches at the Ali Sami Yen stadium?**
a. Galatasaray
b. Fenerbahce
c. Besiktas
d. Al Nassr

92. **Who scored the first goal of France 98?**
a. Rivaldo
b. John Collins
c. Cesar Sampiao
d. Ronaldo

93. **Who won the first ever Champion's League tournament (after it became a group and knockout tournament)?**
a. Ajax
b. AC Milan
c. Marseille
d. Barcelona

94. **From which club did Valencia sign Pablo Aimar?**
a. San Lorenzo
b. Boca Juniors
c. River Plate
d. Racing

95. **Which English club did Rangers beat in the Champions League qualifying rounds in 1992?**
a. Manchester United
b. Blackburn Rovers
c. Arsenal
d. Leeds United

96. **Which club lost to Real Madrid in the first ever European Cup final?**
a. Reims
b. Red Star Belgrade
c. Internazionale
d. Sedan

97. **Which club has the largest stadium in Scotland?**

a. Hibernian

b. Queens Park

c. Celtic

d. Rangers

98.   For which club does Tommy Lovenkrands play?

a. Rangers

b. St Johnstone

c. Hearts

d. Aberdeen

99.   Who was the only player based in Scotland named in the FIFA top 50 players in the world?

a. Henrik Larsson

b. Claudio Caniggia

c. Giovanni Van Bronckhorst

d. Russel Latapy

100.   In which World Cup did Pele first appear?

a. Chile 1962

b. Sweden 1958

c. England 1966

d. Mexico 1970

Answers Round 7

1. John O'Shea
2. Edmilson
3. Saudi Arabia
4. Trevor Sinclair
5. Nelinho
6. Trevor Brooking
7. Ronnie Radford
8. David O'Leary
9. Kieran Richardson
10. Roy Essandoh
11. He was a Seventh Day Adventist and believed the World would end at the turn of the millenium
12. Mart Poom
13. Jose Luis Chilavert
14. Peter Shilton
15. Rene Higuita
16. Dave Beasant
17. David Icke
18. Nick Culkin
19. Sergio Goycochea
20. Jorge Campos
21. Red
22. Claret and Blue
23. Blue and White
24. Notts County, Swansea City, and Juventus
25. Black and White
26. Pale Blue
27. Yellow
28. Red
29. Red, White and Black
30. Dynamo Kiev
31. Elton John
32. Nottingham
33. Jairzinho
34. Aberdeen
35. Goalkeeper
36. Brentford
37. Pink
38. Martin Peters
39. Leeds United
40. Bobby Moore
41. They have all won the English league title with 2 different clubs.
42. Clive Mendonca
43. Pele
44. Dennis Law
45. Niall Quinn
46. Leeds, England
47. Josef Bican, Austria
48. West Ham United
49. James Vaughan - Everton
50. Julie Fleeting

51. Robert Earnshaw

52. Sadio Mané

53. Shane Long - for Southampton against Watford

54. Lionel Messi

55. Real Madrid

56. 1957

57. Kevin Keegan

58. 1968

59. East Stirling, St. Miren, Aberdeen

60. Wolverhampton Wanderers

61. Old 4th

62. Crystal Palace, Stoke City, Leicester City, Charlton Athletic

63. Sheffield Wednesday

64. 23

65. Rochdale United

66. False

67. 20

68. Celtic

69. Queens Park, Vale of Leven

70. TNS LLansantffraid

71. Croydon

72. Leeds United

73. Fiorentina

74. Sliema Wanderers

75. A

76. The Hammer

77. Manchester United

78. 7th

79. Steve McMahon

80. St Etienne

81. Fernando

82. Iceland

83. Aberdeen

84. Argentina

85. Rangers

86. Martin Palermo

87. Missed the kick off after heavy traffic held him up in Glasgow

88. Ali Karimi

89. Christian Abbiati

90. 10

91. Galatasaray

92. Cesar Sampiao

93. Marseille

94. River Plate

95. Leeds United

96. Reims

97. Celtic

98. St Johnstone

99. Russel Latapy

100. Sweden 1958

Printed in Great Britain
by Amazon